NEAPOLITAN MA

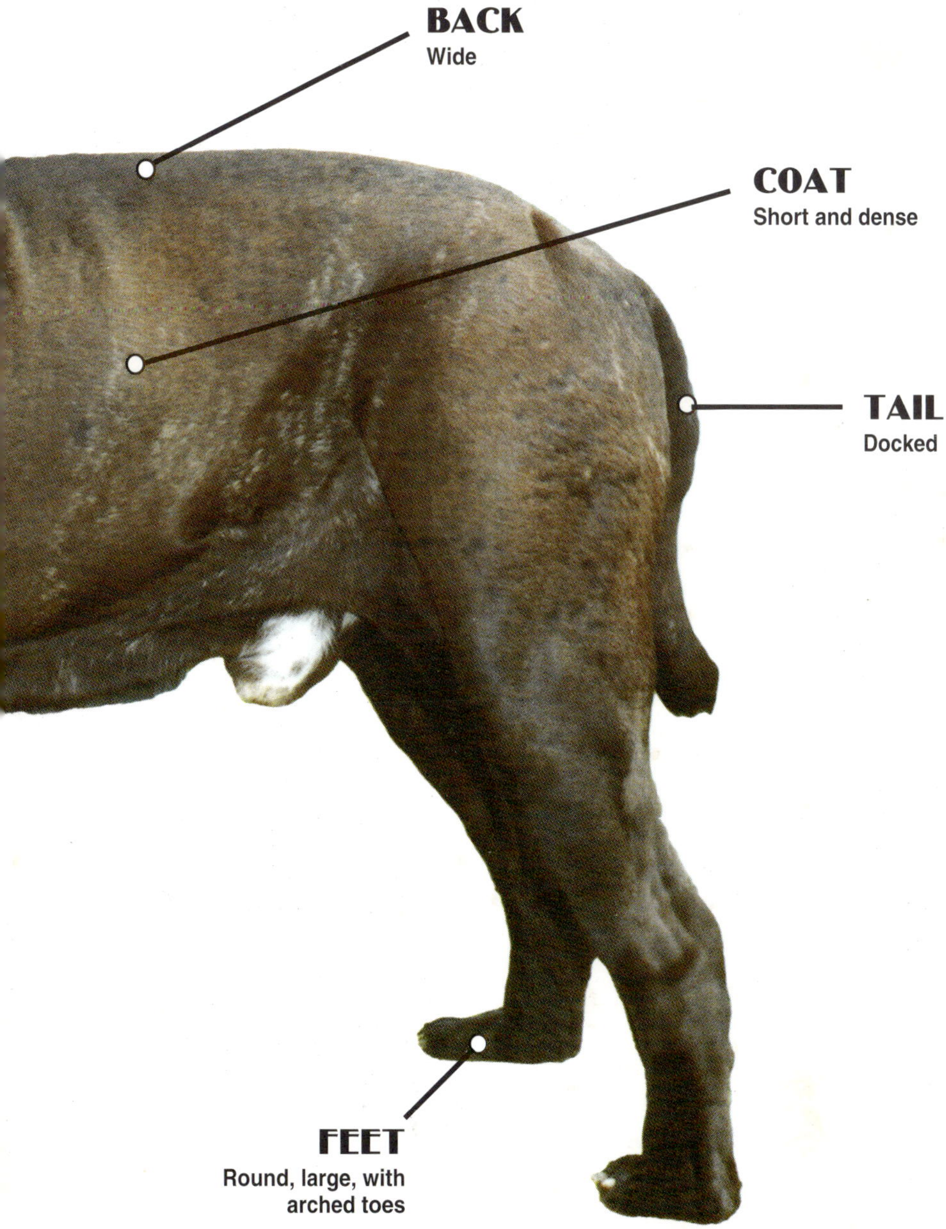
BACK
Wide
COAT
Short and dense
TAIL
Docked
FEET
Round, large, with arched toes

Title page: Neapolitan Mastiff photographed by Isabelle Francais.

Photographers: Paulette Braun, Patricia Care, Rex Davis, J. Deppen, Rene Evans, Isabelle Francais, Robert Gravel, Steve Pleplowski, D. Rappaport, Gonnie Schaffer, R. Sconamiglio, John and Rita Seibel, Alex Smith Photography, Brian Snedeker, Fran and Tom Williams

© T.F.H. Publications, Inc.

Distributed in the UNITED STATES to the Pet Trade by T.F.H. Publications, Inc., 1 TFH Plaza, Neptune City, NJ 07753; on the Internet at www.tfh.com; in CANADA by Rolf C. Hagen Inc., 3225 Sartelon St., Montreal, Quebec H4R 1E8; Pet Trade by H & L Pet Supplies Inc., 27 Kingston Crescent, Kitchener, Ontario N2B 2T6; in ENGLAND by T.F.H. Publications, PO Box 74, Havant PO9 5TT; in AUSTRALIA AND THE SOUTH PACIFIC by T.F.H. (Australia), Pty. Ltd., Box 149, Brookvale 2100 N.S.W., Australia; in NEW ZEALAND by Brooklands Aquarium Ltd., 5 McGiven Drive, New Plymouth, RD1 New Zealand; in SOUTH AFRICA by Rolf C. Hagen S.A. (PTY.) LTD., P.O. Box 201199, Durban North 4016, South Africa; in JAPAN by T.F.H. Publications. Published by T.F.H. Publications, Inc.

MANUFACTURED IN THE
UNITED STATES OF AMERICA
BY T.F.H. PUBLICATIONS, INC.

NEAPOLITAN MASTIFF

A COMPLETE AND RELIABLE HANDBOOK

Robert Gravel and Gonnie Schaffer

RX-134

CONTENTS

History of the Neapolitan Mastiff 7

Characteristics of the Neapolitan Mastiff 10
Grooming • Toys and Treats • Housing

Standard for the Neapolitan Mastiff 18
USNMC Standard

Selecting a Neapolitan Mastiff 24

Your Puppy's New Home 32
On Arriving Home • Dangers in the Home • The First Night •
Other Pets • Housetraining • The Early Days • Identification

Feeding Your Neapolitan Mastiff 42
Factors Affecting Nutritional Needs • Composition and Role
of Food • Amount to Feed

Training Your Neapolitan Mastiff 50
Obedience Training • The Come Command • The Sit Command •
The Heel Command • The Stay Command • The Down
Command • Recall to Heel Command • The No Command

Showing Your Neapolitan Mastiff 66

Breeding and Health Concerns 69
Inbreeding • Linebreeding • Outcrossing • Breeding Based on
Pedigree Alone • Hypothyroidism • Cherry Eye •
Paw Licking Syndrome

Your Healthy Neapolitan Mastiff 78
Physical Exams • Healthy Teeth and Gums • Fighting Fleas •
The Trouble with Ticks • Insects and Other Dangers • Skin
Disorders • Internal Disorders • Worms • Bloat • Vaccinations •
Anesthesia • Axonal Dystrophy • Cancer • Eye Disorders •
Seizures • Accidents

HISTORY OF THE NEAPOLITAN MASTIFF

One look at the Neapolitan Mastiff will send you back in time to an ancient civilization where physical strength and power went hand in hand. When you look at the Neapolitan Mastiff, you see a living antique that can be traced back over 5,000 years. When viewing bits and pieces of sculptures, etchings, and writings scattered across the lands, it is evident that the Neapolitan Mastiff of today has changed only slightly from the dog of ancient times.

When you look at the Neapolitan Mastiff, you see a living antique that can be traced back over 5,000 years. The Mastino of today has changed only slightly from the dog of ancient times. Ch. Justa Call Me Wally, owned by John and Rita Seibel.

HISTORY

After the domestication of livestock, dogs of heavy body and powerful grip were bred by farmers and used as guardians of their flock and for various other functions. These dogs were kept pure in their breeding, in contrast to other breeds that were mixed with the swift, lighter-boned breeds.

We find the ancestors of the Neapolitan Mastiff in lands that were conquered by different people. They were called many names: the Macedonian Dog, Assyrian Dog, Sumerian Molossan, and the Roman Molossus. The names were different, but all were of the same basic type—heavy bodied, with enormous heads, short muzzles, dewlaps, wrinkled foreheads, cropped ears, and heavy legs. Although many Mastiff-type dogs are now extinct, some were saved, such as the Old English Mastiff, or Mastiff, and the Saint Bernard.

It is thought by many that Alexander the Great seeded this large-bodied dog to the lands of his conquest. These dogs were then carried off to war by the Romans and pitted against wild animals such as lions and elephants. To trace the footsteps from this time to 20th-century Italy is a bit sketchy and unclear. This ancient dog seemed to adapt well to the farmers of Italy and was said to be bred in the countryside for many years. The chores of guarding, whether flock, home, or person, were not strange to this noble dog. It seems that there was a certain secrecy to the early breeding of this dog that may have led to his near extinction, or possibly man no longer needed the faithful work that this ancient breed performed.

Although quite obscure at the time, the Neapolitan Mastiff was immediately recognized by Piere Scanziani, a well-known writer and journalist, at a 1946 dog show in Naples, Italy. Scanziani wrote, "I recognized it instantly, it was one of the hundred that Paolo Emilio, the Macedonian, had brought to Rome in his triumph. It was the great dog of Epirus from the height of his centuries, he stared at me imperturbable; his eyes were not hostile, yet not kind. It was a gaze that does not give, yet does not ask anything, it simply contemplates." Piere Scanziani became known as "the father of the breed" and, along with other fanciers of the breed, worked hard to rescue it and cause its current resurgence. A standard to which the dog should be bred was drafted, and the dog became officially recognized by the Italian Kennel Club and the ENCI (Ente Nazionale della Cinofilia Italiana) and

HISTORY

adopted by the FCI (Federation Cynologique Internationale), which is the international organization of which the ENCI is a member. The official name became the Mastino Napoletano, referred to as the Mastino in Italy (later referred to as Mastino worldwide), and nicknamed the "Neo" in the United States. Piere Scanziani purchased a few specimens of this profound breed and his Guaglione1 went on to become the first Italian Champion Neapolitan Mastiff.

Since that time, many other Mastinari (a term that is given to devoted breeders and fanciers) around the world have been instrumental in the advancement of the breed. In the United States, a group of devoted fanciers and breeders formed the United States Neapolitan Mastiff Club (USNMC) and drafted a breed standard to reflect the standard of the country of origin. The standard was approved by the American Kennel Club (AKC) and the Neapolitan Mastiff entered into the AKC foundation stock service (FSS) for pedigree record keeping in 1996. The American Neapolitan Mastiff Association (ANMA) was also formed and is seeking full AKC recognition for our ancient breed here in the United States.

In France, there is Club du Matin Napolitain, and in Mexico, there is a new club called Primer Club del Mastín Napolitano en México. There is also growing popularity in such places as Australia, Switzerland, England, Czech Republic, Sweden, and South America.

A secrecy to the early breeding of the Neapolitan Mastiff may have led to his near extinction. However, Piere Scanziani rediscovered the Mastino in Italy in the 1940s and, along with other fanciers, rescued the breed, resulting in its current resurgence.

CHARACTERISTICS OF THE NEAPOLITAN MASTIFF

The Neapolitan Mastiff is one of the most impressive and remarkable breeds that is in existence today. It is a large breed that can weigh over 150 pounds. In comparison to man or other creatures of a similar weight, the body structure of the Neapolitan Mastiff exemplifies extreme strength, a body type that can perform its function better than any man-made

A large breed that can weigh over 150 pounds, the Neapolitan Mastiff has a body structure that exemplifies extreme physical strength and power.

CHARACTERISTICS

The Mastino's square head, large in comparison to his body, is noted for its ample folds and wrinkles. Ch. Vanguard's Adrianna, owned by Gonnie Schaffer.

machine. His body mass is voluminous, but not fat. His muscular development would cause a game or herding dog to fail at his chores, but for the Neapolitan Mastiff, this is a trade-off he assumed when he chose to be a guardian. His bones are not unlike the trunk of a century-old oak tree—thick, strong, and necessary, or they would surely splinter, causing the massive structure they support to crash to the earth. His body is rectangular in shape when viewed from the side, with the length being longer than the height. This gives him movement similar to a feline, but more like a bear than a canine. This body type combined with good angulation gives him superior reach and allows him to obtain sudden bursts of speed and forward momentum using less energy than a breed with a more square body type. Even though he is efficient in movement for short distances, the Neapolitan Mastiff will tire quickly because of the tremendous amounts of energy needed to move his massive structure.

He is not as tall as the English Mastiff and is somewhere between this breed and the French Mastiff (Dogue De Bordeaux) in size. His tail is docked by one-third and at rest is held down straight or slightly curved like that of a saber.

It is doubtful that there is any other breed of dog whose fundamental characteristics have remained as constant over the centuries as the Neapolitan Mastiff. However, the Neapolitan Mastiff of today shows marked improvements in body and overall squaring of the head, all due to selective breeding. His

CHARACTERISTICS

head is large in comparison to his body, which is noted for its ample folds and wrinkles. His muzzle is also square and short, one-third the length of the whole head. His ears can be cropped or uncropped but are usually cropped for health reasons. (In England, ear cropping is illegal.) He has a captivating and almost intimidating stare, one that would make a foe turn and flee without even a growl. He comes in a variety of colors: gray (blue), black, tawny, and mahogany. The blue is the most common and desired color because of his work as a guardian dog and his ability to blend into the night shadows. He is a working dog originally bred and utilized as a guardian and defender of owner and property. Although bred as a protection dog, he has a steady temperament and is loyal—not outwardly aggressive or apt to bite without reason. Do not confuse the Neapolitan Mastiff with a fighting breed. If you are considering purchasing one with this thought in mind, you will find him far too humble, for he would rather spend his time by your side pleasing you. The Neapolitan Mastiff is certainly not a dog for everyone, but you could not ask for a more faithful companion. He is calm and lumbering and doesn't require constant exercise. The Neapolitan Mastiff is generally good with children, but should always be supervised around them because of his strength and size.

GROOMING

When it comes to grooming, the Neapolitan Mastiff is one of the easiest and most maintenance-free

Although originally bred as a protection dog, the Mastino has a steady temperament and is loyal—not outwardly aggressive or apt to bite without reason. Robert Gravel with two of his dogs, Safira and Pietra.

CHARACTERISTICS

When it comes to grooming, the Neapolitan Mastiff is one of the easiest and most maintenance-free breeds. His hair is short, requires no cutting, and only needs occasional brushing.

breeds. Their hair is short and requires no cutting. Only an occasional brushing is needed. A rubber curry brush or grooming glove works well to remove any dead hair and also brings out the oil in the coat. Although Neapolitan Mastiffs shed very little, the spring tends to be the worst time. While his new coat is growing, don't be alarmed if your dog appears lighter colored and spotted. The older hair that has not fallen off your dog will lighten and the new hair will emerge a darker color. The hair itself is heavy, and what little that does fall out doesn't float around like it can in some breeds.

All things in nature have specific odors associated with them. Just as a rose smells a certain way, a dog has a certain doggie odor. Neapolitan Mastiffs sometimes have a slight musky odor, but this can be removed by bathing with a good dog shampoo. Bathing should be done every other month to keep your dog's coat clean and free of parasites. Some dogs despise getting a bath, while others find it enjoyable.

Start at the dog's face area and clean it with a soaped washcloth, paying particular attention to his chin and any deep folds or wrinkles. Be careful not to

CHARACTERISTICS

get any soap in your dog's eyes. Next, wet his body completely, then apply the soap and scrub well. It is not enough to just wash your dog's back. You must clean his underside, legs, and feet as well. Depending on how dirty he is, you may have to repeat this two or three times. After rinsing, dry your dog with a towel and make sure to dry his ears completely. Many ear infections are caused by moisture left in the ear after bathing. If your dog's ears are uncropped, they need to be cleaned more often to prevent mites and infection. If you notice any red irritated skin in his face folds, you should apply some Panalog to the affected area, which is available from your veterinarian. After bathing, you should wipe a small amount of petroleum jelly on his nose to prevent it from drying out.

Nail cutting should be done with a large nail clipper when they become overgrown. This is not only for aesthetic reasons. If left overgrown, they can cause a young dog to go down on his pasterns. The nail can also become so overgrown that it curls into the pad of the foot. As the nail grows, a bloodline called the quick grows along with it. Be careful not to cut into the quick of the nail, because it will bleed and cause your dog pain. Always keep antiseptic powder on hand to stop the bleeding and prevent infection in case the quick is accidentally cut. Next, use a file to remove any sharp edges. If you are showing your dog, also wipe some petroleum jelly on his nails to give them a shine.

TOYS AND TREATS

Although your dog may quickly destroy most toys, the toys and treats that you choose are important because some items are unsafe. Most squeaky-type toys you see at the store are unsuitable for a Neapolitan Mastiff. Vinyl toys will be torn up in a matter of minutes, and stuffed toys will be unstuffed in seconds. There are a few toys that are relatively safe and will last. The Nylabone® company makes chew bones that are strong and safe. They come in different shapes and flavors such as chicken, ham, and chocolate. Make sure to get one large enough so that your dog does not swallow it whole. The wolf size is good for a puppy and the super size is suitable for an adult. You can throw the bones into the freezer if you have a puppy that is teething. This will make the bone more attractive and will also soothe his gums. The knotted rope bones are also a good choice. They come in different flavors and are washable. The rope will

CHARACTERISTICS

As with all large breeds of dog, it is important to choose toys and treats for your Mastino very carefully—some items may be unsafe due to their small size or lack of durability.

actually floss your dog's teeth as he chews it. Once the rope bone begins to come apart, you should discard it. You should avoid any type of tug rope, because this will teach your dog that it is acceptable to play rough with you.

Rubber toys hold up very well. They come solid or hollow. You must be careful with a toy if it contains a bell inside. Neapolitan Mastiffs have immeasurable patience and they are bound to get it out and swallow it. One rubber toy that stands out is the Kong toy. It's made from pure rubber, is open on both ends, and comes with a one-year guarantee. Rawhide bones, although popular, are not the safest products. When rawhide gets wet, large pieces can be eaten by your dog and block his digestive tract. Natural beef bones are a better choice. They are safer and dogs love them. Natural bones come sterilized or smoked with meat on them, and there are a lot of sizes and shapes to choose from. Putting a piece of cheese or peanut butter inside is sure to create quite a hit. These natural bones also provide minerals for your dog and help keep his teeth free from tartar.

The importance of chew items for your dog cannot be emphasized enough, especially for a puppy. They need these items to chew and to help dislodge baby teeth and cut in the adult teeth. Chewing also helps clean their teeth and will aid in preventing tooth decay and gum disease. Also, by chewing, your dog will

CHARACTERISTICS

have better-smelling breath. If you fail to give them a sufficient number of chew items, they will choose their own—chairs, tables, walls, and outside furniture.

Milk bones are also important for your dog's teeth and gums. Give him at least three of them a day. Try not to give a young puppy too many biscuits, because they can give him diarrhea from the change in diet.

HOUSING

One of the most frequently asked questions concerns the kind of housing that is needed for this large dog. Surprisingly, they don't need two acres of land to wear off their energy. They are just as comfortable with apartment life as they are with a rural home. Just remember you will soon be living with a 120-pound-or-more dog. But you can be assured that once you get past the trail of water from his bowl and that coffee-table-clearing tail, you will find one of the most wonderful, domesticated dogs that exists.

Your dog's new home must be puppy-proofed for him. This consists of making sure that all hazards are removed from the house or out of your puppy's reach. These things include electrical cords, children's toys, houseplants, and clothing. Select a small area in the house and gate it off. This will help in housetraining your dog and keep him out of trouble.

Neapolitan Mastiffs love the outdoors and will enjoy it year round. They will tolerate temperatures as low as zero degrees Fahrenheit, provided they have an insulated dog house, and below zero degrees if the dog house is heated. Bedding in the house could be a blanket (if the dog doesn't rip it to shreds), a pig blanket (the dog won't be able to rip this type of blanket to pieces), or cedar shavings. Straw and hay are undesirable because they hold moisture, which causes fungi to grow and infect your dog.

Although the Mastino will tolerate cold, he does not tolerate heat as well. The preferred dog house for hot climates is made of masonry, because masonry tends to keep cool, provided it's not in sunlight continuously. If you keep your dog in an outside kennel, make sure it is covered or not in direct sunlight. You may want to find a nice, shady tree and construct the kennel near it. This provides plenty of shade and a natural look and feel. Do not use any trees that produce toxic berries or pitted fruit. The kennel should be well constructed with a pipe rail on the bottom to keep the chain link from being bent up. You should also make sure that

CHARACTERISTICS

all the long bolts face outward, so they do not tear a jumping dog's skin. It should be at least 6 feet tall and 120 square feet or larger inside.

There is really no perfect ground cover for inside the kennel. Each has its own advantages and disadvantages. Dirt or grass is the least sanitary and your dog will probably dig holes in the ground. Gravel can be used, but extra care needs to be taken in cleaning and eliminating odors. Concrete is one of the better choices because of its easy cleaning and sanitary properties. If you use concrete, it is necessary to build a small wood platform. Your dog will use this to rest on, preventing damage to his elbows and hindquarters. Once a week the concrete should be treated with a bleach solution or a commercial disinfectant. It is not recommended to house more than one dog in each kennel. Even some female dogs of excellent temperament have been known to quarrel when they are in season. You should also provide each dog with two no-tip water bowls and change the water regularly. One might look at the bowl and think it is half full with water, but upon further examination, you will find it to be filled with an unidentifiable liquid (slime). Fresh water is essential to your Neapolitan Mastiff's well-being.

Neapolitan Mastiffs love the outdoors and will enjoy it year round. Two-year-old Ch. Vanguard's Tristezza, owned by D. Rappaport.

STANDARD FOR THE NEAPOLITAN MASTIFF

The standard was written by Neapolitan Mastiff Club members, breeders, and fanciers in the United States. These members are sworn by their code of ethics to maintain a standard that "reflects the standard of the country of origin." Be sure to check the breed standard in your own country as it may differ.

USNMC STANDARD (AKC-APPROVED)
(*Reprinted with permission from the USNMC.*)

General Appearance—An ancient breed, rediscovered in Italy in the 1940s, the Neapolitan Mastiff is

The essence of the Neapolitan Mastiff is his bestial appearance, astounding head, and imposing size and attitude.

STANDARD

a heavy-boned, massive, awe-inspiring dog bred for use as a guard and defender of owner and property. He is characterized by loose skin, over his entire body, abundant, hanging wrinkles and folds on the head and a voluminous dewlap. The essence of the Neapolitan is his bestial appearance, astounding head and imposing size and attitude. Due to his massive structure, his characteristic movement is rolling and lumbering, not elegant or showy.

Size, Proportion, Substance—A stocky, heavy boned dog, massive in substance, rectangular in proportion. Length of body is 10% - 15% greater than the height at the withers. Height: Dogs: 26 to 31 inches, Bitches: 24 to 29 inches. Average weight of mature Dogs-150 pounds; Bitches-110 pounds; but greater weight is usual and preferable as long as correct proportions and function are maintained.

Disqualifications: Absence of massiveness.

Head—Large in comparison to the body. Differentiated from that of other mastiff breeds by more extensive wrinkling and pendulous lips, which blend into an ample dewlap. Toplines of cranium and the muzzle must be parallel. The face is made up of heavy wrinkles and folds. Required folds are those extending from the outside margin of the eyelids to the dewlap, and from under the lower lids to the outer edges of the lips.

Severe faults: Toplines of the cranium and muzzle not parallel. Disqualifications: Absence of wrinkles and folds.

Expression: Wistful at rest, intimidating when alert. Penetrating stare.

Eyes: Set deep and almost hidden beneath drooping upper lids. Lower lids droop to reveal the haw.

Color: Shades of amber or brown, in accordance with coat color. Pigmentation of the eye rims same as the coat color.

Severe faults: Whitish-blue eyes; depigmentation of the eye rims.

Ears: Set well above the cheekbones. May be cropped or uncropped but are usually cropped to an equilateral triangle for health reasons. If uncropped, they are medium sized, triangular in shape, held tight to the cheeks, and not extending beyond the lower margin of the throat.

Skull: Wide, flat between the ears, slightly arched at the frontal part, and covered with wrinkled skin. The width of the cranium between the cheekbones is

STANDARD

The Mastino's large head is differentiated from that of other mastiff breeds by more extensive wrinkling and pendulous lips, which blend into an ample dewlap.

approximately equal to its length from occiput to stop. The brow is very developed. Frontal furrow is marked. Occiput is barely apparent.

Stop: Very defined, forming a right angle at the junction of muzzle and frontal bones, and then sloping back at a greater angle where the frontal bones meet the frontal furrow of the forehead.

Nose: Large with well-opened nostrils, and in color the same as the coat. The nose is an extension of the top line of the muzzle and should not protrude beyond nor recede behind the front plane of the muzzle.

Severe faults: Depigmentation of the nose.

Muzzle: It is 1/3 the length of the whole head and is as broad as it is long. Viewed from the front, the muzzle is very deep with the outside borders parallel giving it a "squared" appearance. The top plane of the muzzle from stop to tip of nose is straight, but is ridged due to heavy folds of skin covering it.

Severe faults: Top plane of the muzzle curved upward or downward.

Lips: Heavy, thick, and long, the upper lips join beneath the nostrils to form an inverted V. The upper

STANDARD

lips form the lower, outer borders of the muzzle, and the lowest part of these borders is made by the corners of the lips. The corners turn outward to reveal the flews and are in line with the outside corners of the eyes.

Bite: Scissors bite or pincer bite is standard; slight undershot is allowed. Dentition is complete.

Faults: More than 1 missing premolar. Severe faults: Overshot jaw, pronounced undershot jaw which disrupts the outline of the front plane of the muzzle; more than 2 missing teeth.

Neck, Topline and Body—Neck: Slightly arched, rather short, stocky, and well-muscled. The voluminous and well-divided dewlap extends from the lower jaw to the lower neck.

Disqualifications: Absence of dewlap.

Body: The length is 10% - 15% greater than the height of the dog at the withers. Depth of the ribcage

Due to his massive structure, the Mastino's characteristic movement is slow and lumbering. Normal gaits are the walk, trot, gallop, and pace.

STANDARD

is equal to about half the total height of the dog. Ribs are long and well sprung.

Chest: Broad and deep, well muscled. Breast bone is level with the point of the shoulder. **Underline and tuckup:** The underline of the abdomen is practically horizontal. There is little or no tuckup.

Back: Wide. Withers are wide and long, barely rising above the strong topline of the back.

Loin: Well-muscled and harmoniously joined to the back.

Croup: Wide, strong, muscular and slightly sloped. The top of the croup rises slightly and is level with the withers.

Tail: Set gradually toward the tip. It is docked by about 1/3. At rest, the tail hangs straight or in slight S shape. When in action, it is raised to the horizontal or a little higher than the back.

Severe faults: Tail carried straight up or curved over the back. Kinked tail. Disqualifications: Lack of tail or short tail, which is less than 1/3 the length from point of insertion of the tail to the hock.

Forequarters—Heavily built, muscular, and in balance with the hindquarters.

Shoulders: Long, well-muscled, sloping and powerful.

Upper arms: Strongly muscled, powerful. In length, almost 1/3 the height of the dog. **Elbows**: Covered with abundant and loose skin; held parallel to the ribcage, neither tied in nor loose.

Forelegs: Thick, heavy boned, well-muscled, exemplifying strength. About the same length as the upper arms and set well apart.

Pasterns: Thick and flattened from front to back, sloping forward from the leg. **Dewclaws**: Front dewclaws are not removed.

Feet: Round and noticeably large with arched, strong toes. Nails strong, curved and preferably dark-colored. Slight turn out of the front feet is characteristic.

Hindquarters—As a whole, they must be powerful and strong, in harmony with the forequarters.

Thighs: About the same length as the forearms, broad, muscular.

Stifles: Moderate angle, strong.

Legs: Heavy and thick boned, well-muscled. Slightly shorter than the thigh bones. **Hocks**: Powerful and long.

Rear pasterns (metatarsus): Heavy, thick bones.

STANDARD

Viewed from the side, they are perpendicular to the ground. Viewed from the rear, parallel to each other.

Rear dewclaws: Any dewclaws must be removed.

Hind feet: Same as the front feet but slightly smaller.

Coat—The coat is short, dense and of uniform length and smoothness all over the body. The hairs are straight and not longer than 1 inch. No fringe anywhere.

Color—Solid coats of gray (blue), black, mahogany and tawny, and the lighter and darker shades of these colors. All colors may be reverse brindled. There may be solid white markings on the chest, throat area from chin to chest, underside of the body, penis sheath, backs of the pasterns, and on the toes. There may be white hairs at the back of the wrist and around the stopper pad.

Disqualifications: Solid white markings on the head, and extensive solid white markings on any parts of the body not mentioned above.

Gait—The Neapolitan Mastiff's movement is not flashy, but rather slow and lumbering. Normal gaits are the walk, trot, gallop, and pace. The strides are long and elastic, at the same time, powerful, characterized by a long push from the hindquarters and extension of the forelegs. Rolling motion and swaying of the body at all gaits is characteristic. Pacing in the show ring is not to be penalized. Slight paddling movement of the front feet is normal. The head is carried level with or slightly above the back.

Temperament—The Neapolitan Mastiff is steady and loyal to his owner, not aggressive or apt to bite without reason. As a protector of his property and owners, he is always watchful and does not relish intrusion by strangers into his personal space. His attitude is calm yet wary. In the show ring he is majestic and powerful, but not showy.

Faults: The foregoing description is that of the ideal Neapolitan Mastiff. Any deviation from the above described dog must be penalized to the extent of the deviation.

Disqualifications: Absence of massiveness. Absence of wrinkles and folds. Absence of dewlap. Lack of tail or short tail, which is less than 1/3 the length from point of insertion of the tail to the hock. Solid white marks on the head and extensive solid white markings on any parts of the body not mentioned above.

SELECTING A NEAPOLITAN MASTIFF

Before acquiring a new puppy, you must learn what the breed should look like. Pick up a book or two and look at as many pictures as you can find so that you become familiar with the breed. You must also be sure that this is the right time to purchase a dog. You need to give it a lot of thought and consideration. He will become part of your family for years to come. You must consider all his needs, such as housing, grooming, training, feeding, exercise, and health care.

Before deciding to bring your Mastino puppy home, it is important to do your homework and learn as much as you can about the breed.

SELECTING

Ask yourself these questions:

1) Is the puppy going to interfere with my job or other responsibilities?
2) Who is going to housetrain the puppy?
3) What about vacation time? Is there someone who will take care of him while I am gone?
4) Can I provide the proper health care he needs?
5) Is anyone in the household allergic to dogs?
6) Do I have the time to properly train the puppy?

Visit or contact a few reputable breeders, but don't buy the first puppy you see because you think he is cute. All Neapolitan Mastiff puppies are cute. You should take your time and think about it at least overnight. A good Neapolitan Mastiff puppy is one of the more expensive breeds of dog.

Beware of breeders who try to push the puppy on you or a kennel that has three or more litters at the same time. Most of all, don't buy from a breeder because you want to rescue a puppy from bad conditions. A phone call to the proper authorities should be placed instead.

Most breeders will not let you choose your puppy, or they may give you only two puppies to pick from. You must remember that most reputable breeders will breed with the hopes of producing a quality puppy or two that they will keep, which is why the breeding was done in the first place. Also, they usually know the personalities of each puppy and can better match you to the puppy's personality.

If you are allowed to pick your pet puppy, make sure that he looks like a Neapolitan Mastiff, which is what we call breed type. The puppy should be clean, have clear eyes, and be free from any discharge from the nose. Most of all, make sure that he is friendly and outgoing and doesn't back up and cringe in the corner. You may notice a young puppy playfully biting your hand, but don't mistake this for aggression. Young puppies can play very rough, and some breeders separate them as soon as they are weaned to prevent this roughhouse behavior with their littermates.

The puppy should have loose skin draping over his shoulders, a square muzzle, and a wrinkled forehead. He should be plump, well fed, solid, and sound. He should not have thin, weedy legs, tight skin, or a long muzzle.

Let's say that you are interested in a promising show puppy. Some breeders say that they can pick a

SELECTING

The Mastino pup you choose should have loose skin draping over his shoulders, a square muzzle, and a wrinkled forehead.

champion puppy when he is born. This is not so. All they can pick is a show-potential puppy with no faults at that time, but there are many things that can change when a puppy is developing. Between six to ten weeks of age, his eye color may not darken and might remain blue or a shade of blue. Between 4 and 12 months of age, the lower jaw can grow from a scissors bite and become excessively undershot. The puppy's front legs can start to bow. His rear legs can start to hock. His topline can also fall apart; that is, instead of retaining a straight line, he can become sway backed, roach backed, or higher in the rear.

At about one year of age, we know if he has a good front, rear, and topline. We can see if his head is

SELECTING

constructed correctly and if the wrinkling on his head and muzzle is returning, but we still can only hope that his chest will spring and his head will broaden. At this age, we know if he is a promising show puppy. It could take another full year or more for the entire dog to develop. If you are interested in a top-quality show bitch or dog, you should remember that any dog under one year is still a gamble. A promising show puppy can be quite expensive, depending on quality and bloodline.

Now that you have done your research and decided that the Neapolitan Mastiff is right for you, how do you find a reputable breeder? Making this decision should involve a lot of research and questions. As a buyer, you have no real way of telling how your new puppy will develop, so you must rely on the person from whom you will purchase the puppy. There are three options open to you when choosing a puppy. You can buy this puppy from either a puppy store, a backyard breeder, or a hobby/show breeder.

A puppy store will usually know very little background on the puppy, such as temperament, size, and soundness of parents. Most of the time, the owners of the puppy store buy their dogs without seeing them or their parents. The sanitary conditions of puppy stores will also vary. Some places are so clean that they would put a hospital to shame, and yet, there are

Dog ownership is a long-term commitment, so be sure your lifestyle will permit you to fulfill your Neapolitan Mastiff's needs for exercise, training, and companionship.

SELECTING

others that have some serious health violations. Pet stores in the US usually offer health guarantees that will vary from store to store. Most states have laws that commercial puppy sellers must abide by. These laws give you certain rights if your dog is or becomes sick in a specific time period. This is definitely a step in the right direction, but it does not ensure quality. If you are looking for a show/breeding prospect, you had better look elsewhere.

A backyard breeder is a person who thinks it might be fun to breed their dog or is someone who wants to make back the money they spent on their dog. Although their dog may be registered, he probably is only pet quality. Usually the same is true for the stud, chosen because he was the same breed and in the same neighborhood. Although most backyard breeders keep their dogs in clean conditions, very little thought is given to bettering the breed or reducing genetic defects or disease. This type of breeder usually knows very little about the breed.

The serious and dedicated hobby or show breeder is someone who has a love for and an enchantment with the breed. They usually breed to produce the best dogs, giving considerable amounts of money, time, and effort. This person is committed to their breed, and part of this commitment is showing their dogs at dog shows. The knowledgeable breeder will be constantly learning, comparing, and adjusting his or her breeding program. Even if you are not looking for a show prospect, a pet-quality dog will usually be a better value from this type of breeder. The puppy will usually carry all the great qualities as their show littermate but may have a slight defect such as a incorrect bite or light eyes.

Because most reputable breeders exhibit their dogs, a rare breed dog show or a major championship show would be a good place to start your search. When at the show, ask around to see who is breeding, then ask for their phone number or business card. Don't be offended if the breeder is unable to talk to you before the show. Showing a dog requires a person's complete attention and mental preparation. You may also purchase a copy of a dog publication that has classified ads or try contacting the Neapolitan Mastiff club and ask for member breeders.

No two breeders will be exactly alike. Furthermore, they may look for different qualities in their dogs, but they should have some qualifications in common.

SELECTING

Attending a rare breed show in your area is a good way to get information and breeder referrals from Mastino experts and owners. USNMC and Can. Ch. Vanguard's Masero, owned by J. Deppen.

Although it may not be necessary for reputable breeders to meet all these qualifications, the more they meet, the better.

1) The breeder should be a member of a Neapolitan Mastiff Club. This is where he will advance his knowledge in the breed through contacts and publications.

2) The breeder should participate in some form of competition with his dogs. This is a tool of the breeder to judge his dogs and breeding program.

3) The breeder's facilities should be clean and his dogs well socialized and well taken care of. The mother of the litter may not be in top condition from whelping the puppies, but she should still appear clean and healthy.

4) In the US, the breeder should not only give you a verbal guarantee of the puppy's health but should also provide you with a health certificate.

5) The breeder should provide you with copies of the parent's registration papers and those of the puppy, if he has received them. It is common for breeders to use stud dogs from other kennels, but they should be able to provide a copy of his papers and a picture. It is also common for the breeder to require proof of spaying or neutering before providing

SELECTING

actual registration papers on a pet-quality puppy. This is to avoid accidental or poorly planned breeding of their dogs.

6) In the US, the breeder should provide you with a written health guarantee. This guarantee will vary from breeder to breeder, so read it thoroughly and ask questions. Some guarantees may seem outstanding, such as a "lifetime congenital disease" guarantee. In fact, congenital means "born with" and this guarantees only diseases that the dog is born with.

7) The breeder should be knowledgeable about the breed and be able to answer all questions you may ask.

8) The breeder should be willing to take the dog back or to help you place the dog if you can no longer keep him. A reputable breeder is genuinely concerned where his puppy lives and may not only be willing to do this, but may require it in the contract.

9) The breeder should charge a fair price for the puppy, not so low as to cut corners on the care or quality of their dogs.

When you speak to a breeder, it is a good time to ask any questions you may have about the breed, such as temperament or health. Also, feel free to ask about his breeding experience or his breeding stock. A reputable breeder should not be offended by such questions and should welcome your concerns. Write down any questions you may have, such as:

1) What is the personality and temperament of your dogs?

2) Why do you breed Neapolitan Mastiffs? If the answer is money or if it was an accidental breeding, it's best to look elsewhere.

3) What health problems run in the breed and specifically in your lines? What precautions do you take to reduce these problems?

4) What health guarantee do you give on your dogs and for what length of time? (The breeder should also provide a health certificate.)

5) What is in your contract?

6) What type of food do you feed your dogs? Is it a good-quality food that will provide them with proper nutrition?

It is common for a breeder to ask you many questions before selling you a puppy. Although some of these questions may be somewhat personal, they are necessary to ensure that their puppy is going to a good home. Be prepared to answer any of these questions or more.

1) Have you researched the breed and are you familiar with his qualities, good and bad? (If the answer is no, you can expect a lengthy explanation.)

2) Do you have a fenced-in yard and own your own home?

3) Are you looking for a house dog or an outside dog? (Some breeders will not sell you a dog if it is not kept as a house dog.)

4) Do you realize that a pet-quality dog can never be bred and should be neutered or spayed? (If buying a show-potential puppy, the breeder may remain co-owner until the dog is championed or may specify in the contract the number of times the dog must be shown. Expect to pay more for a show-potential puppy.)

5) Do you have other pets or children? (Some breeders may want to visit your home to ensure a proper environment and to see if your children are well behaved.)

Finally, don't be surprised if you are asked what you do for a living. The breeder will want to ensure that you have the ability to provide proper care and medical attention when needed.

For more information on breeder referrals contact the Kennel Club in your area, or in the US contact the following: Peggy Wolfe (USNMC) 630-858-5298 or visit their website at http://www.neapolitan.org/ or contact Robert Gravel (Rockbuster Kennel) 631-667-9078 or Gonnie Schaffer (Vanguard Kennel) 609-561-8657.

Breeders should be knowledgeable about the breed and able to answer all of the questions that you may have. These irresistible seven-week-old Mastino pups are waiting to meet you!

YOUR PUPPY'S NEW HOME

Before actually collecting your puppy, it is better that you purchase the basic items you will need in advance of the pup's arrival date. This allows you more opportunity to shop around and ensure you have exactly what you want rather than having to buy lesser quality in a hurry.

Before your Mastino puppy arrives at his new home, be sure to purchase the basic items he'll need and have a supply of the food he's been eating on hand.

PUPPY'S NEW HOME

It is always better to collect the puppy as early in the day as possible. In most instances this will mean that the puppy has a few hours with your family before it is time to retire for his first night's sleep away from his former home.

If the breeder is local, then you may not need any form of box to place the puppy in when you bring him home. A member of the family can hold the pup in his lap—duly protected by some towels just in case the puppy becomes car sick! Be sure to advise the breeder at what time you hope to arrive for the puppy, as this will obviously influence the feeding of the pup that morning or afternoon. If you arrive early in the day, then they will likely only give the pup a light breakfast so as to reduce the risk of travel sickness.

If the trip will be of a few hours duration, you should take a travel crate with you. The crate will provide your pup with a safe place to lie down and rest during the trip. During the trip, the puppy will no doubt wish to relieve his bowels, so you will have to make a few stops. On a long journey you may need a rest yourself, and can take the opportunity to let the puppy get some fresh air. However, do not let the puppy walk where there may have been a lot of other dogs because he might pick up an infection. Also, if he relieves his bowels at such a time, do not just leave the feces where they were dropped. This is the height of irresponsibility. It has resulted in many public parks and other places actually banning dogs. You can purchase poop-scoops from your pet shop and should have them with you whenever you are taking the dog out where he might foul a public place.

Your journey home should be made as quickly as possible. If it is a hot day, be sure the car interior is amply supplied with fresh air. It should never be too hot or too cold for the puppy. The pup must never be placed where he might be subject to a draft. If the journey requires an overnight stop at a motel, be aware that other guests will not appreciate a puppy crying half the night. You must regard the puppy as a baby and comfort him so he does not cry for long periods. The worst thing you can do is to shout at or smack him. This will mean your relationship is off to a really bad start. You wouldn't smack a baby, and your puppy is still very much just this.

ON ARRIVING HOME

By the time you arrive home the puppy may be

PUPPY'S NEW HOME

Although it's tempting, do not introduce your Mastino puppy to friends and neighbors for at least 48 hours, especially if he's not fully vaccinated. He needs time to adjust to his new environment and to build up his immunities.

very tired, in which case he should be taken to his sleeping area and allowed to rest. Children should not be allowed to interfere with the pup when he is sleeping. If the pup is not tired, he can be allowed to investigate his new home—but always under your close supervision. After a short look around, the puppy will no doubt appreciate a light meal and a drink of water. Do not overfeed him at his first meal because he will be in an excited state and more likely to be sick.

Although it is an obvious temptation, you should not invite friends and neighbors around to see the new arrival until he has had at least 48 hours in which to settle down. Indeed, if you can delay this longer then do so, especially if the puppy is not fully vaccinated. At the very least, the visitors might introduce some local bacteria on their clothing that the puppy is not immune to. This aspect is always a risk when a pup has been moved some distance, so the fewer people the pup meets in the first week or so the better.

DANGERS IN THE HOME

Your home holds many potential dangers for a little mischievous puppy, so you must think about these in advance and be sure he is protected from them. The more obvious are as follows:

PUPPY'S NEW HOME

Open Fires. All open fires should be protected by a mesh screen guard so there is no danger of the pup being burned by spitting pieces of coal or wood.

Electrical Wires. Puppies just love chewing on things, so be sure that all electrical appliances are neatly hidden from view and are not left plugged in when not in use. It is not sufficient simply to turn the plug switch to the off position—pull the plug from the socket.

Open Doors. A door would seem a pretty innocuous object, yet with a strong draft it could kill or injure a puppy easily if it is slammed shut. Always ensure there is no risk of this happening. It is most likely during warm weather when you have windows or outside doors open and a sudden gust of wind blows through.

Balconies. If you live in a high-rise building, obviously the pup must be protected from falling. Be sure he cannot get through any railings on your patio, balcony, or deck.

Ponds and Pools. A garden pond or a swimming pool is a very dangerous place for a little puppy to be near. Be sure it is well screened so there is no risk of the pup falling in. It takes barely a minute for a pup—or a child—to drown.

Your home presents many potential dangers to a young puppy, like this unfenced area, so be sure to puppy-proof your house and yard to keep your curious Mastino from harm.

PUPPY'S NEW HOME

The Kitchen. While many puppies will be kept in the kitchen, at least while they are toddlers and not able to control their bowel movements, this is a room full of danger—especially while you are cooking. When cooking, keep the puppy in a play pen or in another room where he is safely out of harm's way. Alternatively, if you have a carry box or crate, put him in this so he can still see you but is well protected.

Be aware, when using washing machines, that more than one puppy has clambered in and decided to have a nap and received a wash instead! If you leave the washing machine door open and leave the room for any reason, then be sure to check inside the machine before you close the door and switch on.

Small Children. Toddlers and small children should never be left unsupervised with puppies. In spite of such advice it is amazing just how many people not only do this but also allow children to pull and maul pups. They should be taught from the outset that a puppy is not a plaything to be dragged about the home—and they should be promptly scolded if they disobey.

Children must be shown how to lift a puppy so it is safe. Failure by you to correctly educate your children about dogs could one day result in their getting a very nasty bite or scratch. When a puppy is lifted, his weight must always be supported. To lift the pup, first place your right hand under his chest. Next, secure the pup by using your left hand to hold his neck. Now you can lift him and bring him close to your chest. Never lift a pup by his ears and, while he can be lifted by the scruff of his neck where the fur is loose, there is no reason ever to do this, so don't.

Beyond the dangers already cited you may be able to think of other ones that are specific to your home—steep basement steps or the like. Go around your home and check out all potential problems—you'll be glad you did.

THE FIRST NIGHT

The first few nights a puppy spends away from his mother and littermates are quite traumatic for him. He will feel very lonely, maybe cold, and will certainly miss the heartbeat of his siblings when sleeping. To help overcome his loneliness it may help to place a clock next to his bed—one with a loud tick. This will in some way soothe him, as the clock ticks to a rhythm not dissimilar from a heartbeat. A cuddly toy may also

PUPPY'S NEW HOME

On his first night in his new home, your little Mastino may be missing the company of his mother and littermates. Giving him some extra attention will help him to overcome his loneliness.

help in the first few weeks. A dim nightlight may provide some comfort to the puppy, because his eyes will not yet be fully able to see in the dark. The puppy may want to leave his bed for a drink or to relieve himself.

If the pup does whimper in the night, there are two things you should not do. One is to get up and chastise him, because he will not understand why you are shouting at him; and the other is to rush to comfort him every time he cries because he will quickly realize that if he wants you to come running all he needs to do is to holler loud enough!

By all means give your puppy some extra attention on his first night, but after this quickly refrain from so doing. The pup will cry for a while but then settle down and go to sleep. Some pups are, of course, worse than others in this respect, so you must use balanced judgment in the matter. Many owners take their pups to bed with them, and there is certainly nothing wrong with this.

The pup will be no trouble in such cases. However, you should only do this if you intend to let this be a permanent arrangement, otherwise it is hardly fair to the puppy. If you have decided to have two puppies, then they will keep each other company and you will have few problems.

OTHER PETS

If you have other pets in the home then the puppy must be introduced to them under careful supervision. Puppies will get on just fine with any other pets—

PUPPY'S NEW HOME

but you must make due allowance for the respective sizes of the pets concerned, and appreciate that your puppy has a rather playful nature. It would be very foolish to leave him with a young rabbit. The pup will want to play and might bite the bunny and get altogether too rough with it. Kittens are more able to defend themselves from overly cheeky pups, who will get a quick scratch if they overstep the mark. The adult cat could obviously give the pup a very bad scratch, though generally cats will jump clear of pups and watch them from a suitable vantage point. Eventually they will meet at ground level where the cat will quickly hiss and box a puppy's ears. The pup will soon learn to respect an adult cat; thereafter they will probably develop into great friends as the pup matures into an adult dog.

HOUSETRAINING

Undoubtedly, the first form of training your puppy will undergo is in respect to his toilet habits. To achieve this you can use either newspaper, or a large litter tray filled with soil or lined with newspaper. A puppy cannot control his bowels until he is a few months old, and not fully until he is an adult. Therefore you must anticipate his needs and be prepared for a few accidents. The prime times a pup will urinate and defecate are shortly after he wakes up from a sleep, shortly after he has eaten, and after he has been playing awhile. He will usually whimper and start searching the room for a suitable place. You must quickly pick him up and place him on the newspaper or in the litter tray. Hold him in position gently but firmly. He might jump out of the box without doing anything on the first one or two occasions, but if you simply repeat the procedure every time you think he wants to relieve himself then eventually he will get the message.

When he does defecate as required, give him plenty of praise, telling him what a good puppy he is. The litter tray or newspaper must, of course, be cleaned or replaced after each use—puppies do not like using a dirty toilet any more than you do. The pup's toilet can be placed near the kitchen door and as he gets older the tray can be placed outside while the door is open. The pup will then start to use it while he is outside. From that time on, it is easy to get the pup to use a given area of the yard.

Many breeders recommend the popular alternative of crate training. Upon bringing the pup home, introduce him to his crate. The open wire crate is the best choice, placed in a restricted, draft-free area of the home. Put

Opposite: Take your Mastino puppy outside to relieve himself after eating, sleeping, and playing. Remember to use positive reinforcement and praise, which are important parts of the housetraining process.

PUPPY'S NEW HOME

PUPPY'S NEW HOME

the pup's Nylabone® and other favorite toys in the crate along with a wool blanket or other suitable bedding. The puppy's natural cleanliness instincts prohibit him from soiling in the place where he sleeps, his crate. The puppy should be allowed to go in and out of the open crate during the day, but he should sleep in the crate at the night and at other intervals during the day. Whenever the pup is taken out of his crate, he should be brought outside (or to his newspapers) to do his business. Never use the crate as a place of punishment. You will see how quickly your pup takes to his crate, considering it as his own safe haven from the big world around him.

THE EARLY DAYS

You will no doubt be given much advice on how to bring up your puppy. This will come from dog-owning friends, neighbors, and through articles and books you may read on the subject. Some of the advice will be sound, some will be nothing short of rubbish. What you should do above all else is to keep an open mind and let common sense prevail over prejudice and worn-out ideas that have been handed down over the centuries. There is no one way that is superior to all others, no more than there is no one dog that is exactly a replica of another. Each is an individual and must always be regarded as such.

A dog never becomes disobedient, unruly, or a menace to society without the full consent of his owner. Your puppy may have many limitations, but the singular biggest limitation he is confronted with in so many instances is his owner's inability to understand his needs and how to cope with them.

IDENTIFICATION

It is a sad reflection on our society that the number of dogs and cats stolen every year runs into many thousands. To these can be added the number that get lost. If you do not want your cherished pet to be lost or stolen, then you should see that he is carrying a permanent identification number, as well as a temporary tag on his collar.

Permanent markings come in the form of tattoos placed either inside the pup's ear flap, or on the inner side of a pup's upper rear leg. The number given is then recorded with one of the national registration companies. Research laboratories will not purchase dogs carrying numbers as they realize these are clearly

PUPPY'S NEW HOME

someone's pet, and not abandoned animals. As a result, thieves will normally abandon dogs so marked and this at least gives the dog a chance to be taken to the police or the dog pound, when the number can be traced and the dog reunited with its family. The only problem with this method at this time is that there are a number of registration bodies, so it is not always apparent which one the dog is registered with (as you provide the actual number). However, each registration body is aware of his competitors and will normally be happy to supply their addresses. Those holding the dog can check out which one you are with. It is not a perfect system, but until such is developed it's the best available.

Another permanent form of identification is the microchip, a computer chip that is no bigger than a grain of rice that is injected between the dog's shoulder blades. The dog feels no discomfort. The dog also receives a tag that says he is microchipped. If the dog is lost and picked up by the humane society, they can trace the owner by scanning the microchip. It is the safest form of identification.

A temporary tag takes the form of a metal or plastic disk large enough for you to place the dog's name and your phone number on it—maybe even your address as well. In virtually all places you will be required to obtain a license for your puppy. This may not become applicable until the pup is six months old, but it might apply regardless of his age. Much depends upon the state within a country, or the country itself, so check with your veterinarian if the breeder has not already advised you on this.

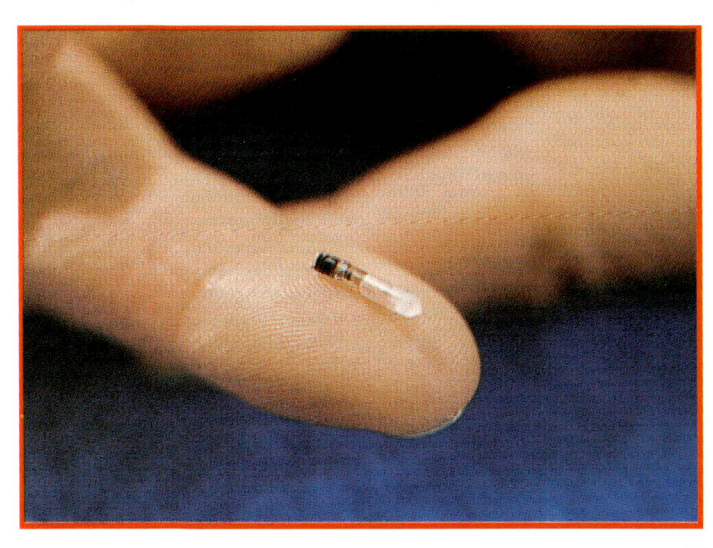

If your Mastino is lost, a form of identification can aid in his safe return. The newest and safest method used is the microchip, which is permanently injected under the dog's skin.

FEEDING YOUR NEAPOLITAN MASTIFF

After you have purchased your new puppy, whether he is show or companion quality, proper feeding is imperative if you want your pup to develop properly. A premium quality food with a moderate protein level and a high amount of fat should be chosen. When selecting a dog food, make sure to look at the nutritional label on the product. Because the Neapolitan Mastiff is essentially a carnivore, this food should have meat or poultry as the first ingredient. This means that meat or poultry is in higher quantity than any other ingredient. It should have balanced vitamins and minerals and be naturally preserved. Actual

Good nutrition is imperative if you want your Mastino puppy to develop properly.

feeding tests should also have been performed using AAFCO procedures (some poorer quality foods may only be formulated to meet AAFCO nutritional requirements).

Puppies under 12 weeks of age should be fed 3 times a day, then reduce the feeding to 2 times a day. You may need to adjust the diet of a growing dog to account for growth spurts and activity. Also, half the amount of food fed should be fresh cooked meat, such as chicken or beef.

The adult Neapolitan Mastiff can consume up to a gallon of food a day. It is not recommended to overfeed or oversupplement your dog, especially puppies or young adults. Too much weight or proteins and minerals can actually cause damage to your dog's tendons, ligaments, and skeletal structure and may aid in bringing on diseases like hip dysplasia. Although hip dysplasia is a genetic condition, it is directly influenced by environmental conditions such as excess body weight and over-exercising. Clinical studies show that by reducing the weight of young puppies, you can reduce the incidence of hip dysplasia. Just by the nature of the breed, a Neapolitan Mastiff puppy is born carrying too much weight for his young body. It is important to keep his weight correct until his bone structure is fully developed. By doing so, your Neapolitan Mastiff puppy will grow slowly and still attain his maximum weight once mature. Remember to let the puppy exercise to stress the bones so that they will develop.

Neapolitan Mastiffs can make quite a mess at feeding time. Their heavy lips and dewlap collect food while eating and leave a trail to the water bowl, then soak up water while drinking and leave a trail back to the food bowl. Some owners feed their dog on a tile floor that provides for easy cleaning. If daily cleaning is a problem, a better idea would be to feed him outside on a deck or patio.

NUTRITION

Dog owners today are fortunate in that they live in an age when considerable cash has been invested in the study of canine nutritional requirements. This means dog food manufacturers are very concerned about ensuring that their foods are of the best quality. The result of all of their studies, apart from the food itself, is that dog owners are bombarded with advertisements telling them why they must pur-

FEEDING

chase a given brand. The number of products available to you is unlimited, so it is hardly surprising to find that dogs in general suffer from obesity and an excess of vitamins, rather than the reverse. Be sure to feed age-appropriate food—puppy food up to one year of age, adult food thereafter. Generally breeders recommend dry food supplemented by canned, if needed.

FACTORS AFFECTING NUTRITIONAL NEEDS

Activity Level. A dog that lives in a country environment and is able to exercise for long periods of the day will need more food than the same breed of dog living in an apartment and given little exercise.

Quality of the Food. Obviously the quality of food will affect the quantity required by a puppy. If the nutritional content of a food is low then the puppy will need more of it than if a better quality food was fed.

Balance of Nutrients and Vitamins. Feeding a puppy the correct balance of nutrients is not easy because the average person is not able to measure out ratios of one to another, so it is a case of trying to see that nothing is in excess. However, only tests, or your veterinarian, can be the source of reliable advice.

Genetic and Biological Variation. Apart from all of the other considerations, it should be remem-

Although the adult Neapolitan Mastiff can consume up to a gallon of food a day, be careful not to overfeed or oversupplement your dog—it can be hazardous to his health.

FEEDING

The amount of exercise your Mastino receives affects his food intake. A very active dog will require more to eat than a less active dog of the same size.

bered that each puppy is an individual. His genetic make-up will influence not only his physical characteristics but also his metabolic efficiency. This being so, two pups from the same litter can vary quite a bit in the amount of food they need to perform the same function under the same conditions. If you consider the potential combinations of all of these factors then you will see that pups of a given breed could vary quite a bit in the amount of food they will need. Before discussing feeding quantities it is valuable to know at least a little about the composition of food and its role in the body.

COMPOSITION AND ROLE OF FOOD

The main ingredients of food are protein, fats, and carbohydrates, each of which is needed in relatively large quantities when compared to the other needs of vitamins and minerals. The other vital ingredient of food is, of course, water. Although all foods obviously contain some of the basic ingredients needed for an animal to survive, they do not all contain the ingredients in the needed ratios or type. For example, there are many forms of protein, just as there are many types of carbohydrates. Both of these compounds are found in meat and in vegetable matter—but not

FEEDING

all of those that are needed will be in one particular meat or vegetable. Plants, especially, do not contain certain amino acids that are required for the synthesis of certain proteins needed by dogs.

Likewise, vitamins are found in meats and vegetable matter, but vegetables are a richer source of most. Meat contains very little carbohydrates. Some vitamins can be synthesized by the dog, so do not need to be supplied via the food. Dogs are carnivores and this means their digestive tract has evolved to need a high quantity of meat as compared to humans. The digestive system of carnivores is unable to break down the tough cellulose walls of plant matter, but it is easily able to assimilate proteins from meat.

In order to gain its needed vegetable matter in a form that it can cope with, the carnivore eats all of its prey. This includes the partly digested food within the stomach. In commercially prepared foods, the cellulose is broken down by cooking. During this process the vitamin content is either greatly reduced or lost altogether. The manufacturer therefore adds vitamins once the heat process has been completed. This is why commercial foods are so useful as part of a feeding regimen, providing they are of good quality and from a company that has prepared the foods very carefully.

Proteins

These are made from amino acids, of which at least ten are essential if a puppy is to maintain healthy growth. Proteins provide the building blocks for the puppy's body. The richest sources are meat, fish and poultry, together with their by-products. The latter will include milk, cheese, yogurt, fishmeal, and eggs. Vegetable matter that has a high protein content includes soy beans, together with numerous corn and other plant extracts that have been dehydrated. The actual protein content needed in the diet will be determined both by the activity level of the dog and his age. The total protein need will also be influenced by the digestibility factor of the food given.

Fats

These serve numerous roles in the puppy's body. They provide insulation against the cold, and help buffer the organs from knocks and general activity shocks. They provide the richest source of energy, and reserves of this, and they are vital in the transport

FEEDING

Your Neapolitan Mastiff should have a healthy, well-balanced diet that includes the proper amount of proteins, fats, and carbohydrates.

of vitamins and other nutrients, via the blood, to all other organs. Finally, it is the fat content within a diet that gives it palatability. It is important that the fat content of a diet should not be excessive. This is because the high energy content of fats (more than twice that of protein or carbohydrate) will increase the overall energy content of the diet. The puppy will adjust its food intake to that of its energy needs, which are obviously more easily met in a high-energy diet. This will mean that while the fats are providing the energy needs of the puppy, the overall diet may not be providing its protein, vitamin, and mineral needs, so signs of protein deficiency will become apparent. Rich sources of fats are meat, their byproducts (butter, milk), and vegetable oils, such as safflower, olive, corn or soy bean.

Carbohydrates

These are the principal energy compounds given to puppies and adult dogs. Their inclusion within most commercial brand dog foods is for cost, rather than dietary needs. These compounds are more commonly known as sugars, and they are seen in simple or

FEEDING

complex compounds of carbon, hydrogen, and oxygen. One of the simple sugars is called glucose, and it is vital to many metabolic processes. When large chains of glucose are created, they form complex sugars. One of these is called glycogen, and it is found in the cells of animals. Another, called starch, is the material that is found in the cells of plants.

Vitamins

These are not foods as such but chemical compounds that assist in all aspects of an animal's life. They help in so many ways that to attempt to describe these effectively would require a chapter in itself. Fruits are a rich source of vitamins, as is the liver of most animals. Many vitamins are unstable and easily destroyed by light, heat, moisture, or rancidity. An excess of vitamins, especially A and D, has been proven to be very harmful. Provided a puppy is receiving a balanced diet, it is most unlikely there will be a deficiency, whereas hypervitaminosis (an excess of vitamins) has become quite common due to owners and breeders feeding unneeded supplements. The only time you should feed extra vitamins to your puppy is if your veterinarian advises you to.

Minerals

These provide strength to bone and cell tissue, as well as assist in many metabolic processes. Examples are calcium, phosphorous, copper, iron, magnesium, selenium, potassium, zinc, and sodium. The recommended amounts of all minerals in the diet has not been fully established. Calcium and phosphorous are known to be important, especially to puppies. They help in forming strong bone. As with vitamins, a mineral deficiency is most unlikely in pups given a good and varied diet. Again, an excess can create problems—this applying equally to calcium.

Water

This is the most important of all nutrients, as is easily shown by the fact that the adult dog is made up of about 60 percent water, the puppy containing an even higher percentage. Dogs must retain a water balance, which means that the total intake should be balanced by the total output. The intake comes either by direct input (the tap or its equivalent), plus water released when food is oxidized, known as metabolic water (remember that all foods contain the elements hydrogen and oxygen that

FEEDING

recombine in the body to create water). A dog without adequate water will lose condition more rapidly than one depleted of food, a fact common to most animal species.

AMOUNT TO FEED

The best way to determine dietary requirements is by observing the puppy's general health and physical appearance. If he is well covered with flesh, shows good bone development and muscle, and is an active alert puppy, then his diet is fine. A puppy will consume about twice as much as an adult (of the same breed). You should ask the breeder of your puppy to show you the amounts fed to their pups and this will be a good starting point.

The puppy should eat his meal in about five to seven minutes. Any leftover food can be discarded or placed into the refrigerator until the next meal (but be sure it is thawed fully if your fridge is very cold).

If the puppy quickly devours its meal and is clearly still hungry, then you are not giving him enough food. If he eats readily but then begins to pick at it, or walks away leaving a quantity, then you are probably giving him too much food. Adjust this at the next meal and you will quickly begin to appreciate what the correct amount is. If, over a number of weeks, the pup starts to look fat, then he is obviously overeating; the reverse is true if he starts to look thin compared with others of the same breed.

The best way to determine if your puppy's diet is sufficient is by checking his bone and muscle development, his weight, and his level of activity.

TRAINING YOUR NEAPOLITAN MASTIFF

Training your Neapolitan Mastiff should be a top priority. An untrained dog may not only be a nuisance in your household, but could also be a menace to society. Just imagine a 150-pound Neapolitan Mastiff, not housetrained, jumping on you, your family, and the kitchen table. Your unsocialized dog is afraid of everybody and feels that your guests are threats to his life and refuses to let them in. He thinks you are weak and is unwilling to obey or respond to any of your

Because of his massive size, training your Neapolitan Mastiff should be a top priority. Four-year-old Urano Della Zacchera, owned by Rene Evans.

TRAINING

commands. He rips up your yard and furniture, and to top it off, he bit your neighbor while you were chatting on Sunday morning. Although not many people would let their dog get this out of hand, we hope this scenario is compelling enough for you to make the time and take training seriously. If you still don't believe that proper training is important, you should reconsider bringing a Neapolitan Mastiff into your home.

As stated earlier, the first type of training that your Neapolitan Mastiff receives should be housetraining. Housetraining your dog will require repetitive training and constant observation. Housetraining can start as young as six weeks of age, although eight weeks may be more practical. If your puppy is paper trained, try to switch him to outside training as quickly as possible. Select a spot outside and take your puppy exclusively to that area while he is on a leash or lead. When your puppy eliminates in that spot, make sure to praise him. Avoid playing with him and let him know that he is there for only one reason. Try to use words like "out" or "go out" to associate with his housetraining. Also, make sure to keep the area clean or your dog may refuse to go there. Housetraining time will vary with each dog. There have been instances in which one littermate was housetrained in days, and the other had intermittent accidents for months.

Crate training is the easiest and fastest way to housetrain your Mastino. Putting him in a crate can also keep him safe and out of trouble when he's not being supervised.

TRAINING

A few key times to take your puppy out are first thing in the morning, after naps, after meals, and before bed. If you catch your dog in the "act," correct him with a firm "no" and take him outside to his area. If you don't catch him, it is too late to correct him at this time, because he will not know why he is being yelled at. If your dog has an accident in the house, you need to remove the odor from the floor or carpeting. Household cleaners or ammonia will not do the trick. You need to use a stain and odor remover that contains natural enzymes that breaks down the stain and eliminates the smell. This type of product can be purchased at your pet store.

A dog crate is not only helpful with housetraining, but can keep your dog safe and out of trouble when he is not supervised. A crate can also prevent destructive behavior in the house when you are not at home. Just as you shouldn't let a human child crawl around your home and injure himself, the same is true for your puppy. It is confusing that parents who confine their infant to a playpen, walker, or crib for safety will say that they feel funny or cruel protecting their new eight-week-old puppy in the same manner. What is cruel is allowing an innocent puppy to swallow a foreign object and die or become destructive and then wind up at the local animal shelter when all this can be avoided. Only a short period of training can bring a lifetime of pleasure and companionship with your canine friend.

Believed to descend from wolves, it is instinctive for dogs to keep their kennel clean, just as it is for the wolves to keep their den clean and not eliminate in it. Dogs actually feel comfortable in this den-type home. Fake sheepskin is a great product for your dog to sleep on in the crate. It's soft, washable, and does not unravel like other fabric or carpet. You need to place your dog's crate in a spot where he can still be part of the family and introduce him to the crate for short periods at a time. At first he may cry out, but do not give in to his wishes. Try to get your dog used to a crate at a young age, because there isn't a crate built that can hold a full-grown Neapolitan Mastiff when he wants out.

Besides housetraining there are two types of training we would recommend for a young Neapolitan Mastiff: leash or lead training and socialization. Leash or lead training should begin by placing a nylon weave collar around your dog's neck and letting him drag the leash

TRAINING

Your Mastino must learn to accept a collar and leash for his safety and the safety of others.

around the floor while he is supervised. At first, he may be uncomfortable with this new feeling, but he will soon become accustomed to it. After he gets used to this, you can then let him walk around on a loose lead. Then try to stand in front of your puppy and call him while holding the end of the leash. In a short time, your new puppy should be walking by your side.

A choke collar and leather lead may be used next to walk your dog. With your dog facing you, hold the collar in the form of a "P" and place it over your dog's head. If you put a choke on backward, it will not release from around your dog's neck. Place the leather lead on your right thumb and loop it up. Then walk your dog on your left side supporting the lead with your left hand. A slight jerk and release can be used while walking to help slow him down and when turning. If your Neapolitan Mastiff has natural ears, you may want to use a nylon choke so that his ears don't get pinched in the chain. If you have an adult dog that has never been leash trained, you may want to use a pinch or prong collar during your training

TRAINING

sessions. Because of their mass and forward moment, do not expect a Neapolitan Mastiff to make quick turns or stop like most breeds can. When you are done walking or training your dog, remember to take the choke collar off. If your dog jumps up and this collar gets caught on something, it can injure or even kill him.

A leash and choke collar can also be used for corrective training and basic obedience training. Basic obedience can be started at about three months of age or after the puppy has had his vaccinations. A Neapolitan Mastiff must be corrected firmly when he has done something wrong. When we say firm correction, it does not mean screaming at or beating your dog. You must use a word like "no" and repeat it in a firm, authoritative voice. Constant yelling or hitting your dog will certainly take away his noble attitude and eventually break him of his will.

One of the most important things that you can do while training your Neapolitan Mastiff is to offer him ample time to socialize. People quite often say, "I want my dog to guard me and my family, so when I have company over I hide him away and I also tell him to "sick 'em" when we see people." This is one of the biggest mistakes an owner of a Neapolitan Mastiff can make. If a dog is not socialized properly, he will be afraid of people, become a fear biter, and possibly hurt someone without reason. A Neapolitan Mastiff should never bite without reason. As an adult dog, he will guard you and his domain with proper judgment as he has done for thousands of years if he is correctly socialized.

A breeder must never sell a Neapolitan Mastiff to any person who strictly wants a guard dog, nor should one ever be purchased for this reason. The first and foremost function of the Neapolitan Mastiff of today is to be a member of the family and a companion. Second, he should be a proper member of society. Only when he has met the first two criteria and has been trained properly and socialized can he be used to protect you and your family.

Socialization should start first at home and then, after your vet's permission, in public. Studies show that dogs develop these skills very young in life, so it is important to purchase a well-socialized puppy and to contunue his training. When people come to visit, make your dog sit and have the visitors pet him and give him a treat. Don't forget to praise your dog to let him know that you're happy with his behavior.

TRAINING

As soon as your Mastino is old enough, take him with you wherever you go. Introducing him to new people, places, and experiences will ensure that your dog is well-socialized.

A puppy should be enrolled in a puppy kindergarten class where he will meet many new puppies and people. It is a wonderful start for a new puppy to learn how to become a good citizen. The instructor will also show you some basic training techniques and tips. Make sure that your puppy has all of his shots before taking him around other dogs.

Get your puppy used to the car by taking him on short trips around the block, gradually increasing the length of time he is in the car. A trip to the park for some fun is a wonderful way for your dog to meet new people and experience new things. There is nothing like a little playing to get that shy puppy out of his shell.

Again, it is necessary to say that this training must be done. If you are unwilling, unable, or cannot find the time to train your dog properly, you might want to consider a smaller breed. Not that a smaller breed will be easier to train, but a small untrained dog will be, by virtue or his size, less of a danger and menace to society. This is not said out of love for training, but to warn the careless owner of the damage and destruction an untrained or wrongly trained large breed such as the Neapolitan Mastiff can cause. If he is properly

TRAINING

bred, trained, and socialized, he will be a loving and loyal companion for life.

A few words of caution for anyone who is considering attack-training a Neapolitan Mastiff—don't do it. You may easily find yourself involved in a serious lawsuit. The Neapolitan Mastiff is not and never should be used as an attack dog. He is a guardian and protector, not an aggressor. His instinct to bite is in a sleep state, but once awakened (forced to attack-train), he may always bite, no matter who it is.

Some people say that the "true" dog is being turned into a gentle giant. These people use cruel methods like chaining their dogs to the ground on four-inch chains to build up their chests or beating them with sticks to bring out their true aggression. They seem to think that this will cause some kind of genetic regression to the primitive Mastiff. Aside from making their dog socially unfit or even insane, all they will accomplish is to incite a survival instinct that exists in all creatures, even man—kill or be killed. Anyone with a basic knowledge of genetics will know that environment has a huge influence on temperament. To select for temperament in either direction will have but a small influence on future generations. Also, by taking a dog with a genetic makeup for a stable temperament and making him vicious and insane will not change the genetic makeup of his offspring. As you can see, these people are misinformed, misguided, and need to be stopped before they damage the good and noble reputation that this breed currently has.

OBEDIENCE TRAINING

Once your puppy has settled into your home and responds to his name, then you can begin his basic obedience training. Before giving advice on how you should go about doing this, two important points should be made. You should train the puppy in isolation of any potential distractions, and you should keep all lessons very short. It is essential that you have the full attention of your puppy. This is not possible if there are other people about, or televisions and radios on, or other pets in the vicinity. Even when the pup has become a young adult, the maximum time you should allocate to a lesson is about 20 minutes. However, you can give the puppy more than one lesson a day, three being as many as are recommended, each well spaced apart.

TRAINING

Before beginning a lesson, always play a little game with the puppy so he is in an active state of mind and thus more receptive to the matter at hand. Likewise, always end a lesson with fun-time for the pup, and always—this is most important—end on a high note, praising the puppy. Let the lesson end when the pup has done as you require so he receives lots of fuss. This will really build his confidence.

THE COME COMMAND

Come is the most vital of all commands and especially so for the independently minded dog. To teach the puppy to come, let him reach the end of a long lead, then give the command and his name, gently pulling him toward you at the same time. As soon as he associates the word come with the action of moving toward you, pull only when he does not respond immediately. As he starts to come, move back to make him learn that he must come from a distance as well as when he is close to you. Soon you may be able to practice without a leash, but if he is slow to come or notably disobedient, go to him and pull him toward you, repeating the command. Never scold a dog during this exercise—or any other exercise. Remember the trick is that the puppy must want to come to you. For the very independent dog, hand signals may work better than verbal commands.

Keep training sessions short and always remember to praise your Mastino when he obeys a command—ending on a high note will build his confidence.

TRAINING

The sit is the foundation command for everything else your dog will learn. Six-month-old Rockbuster Vanguard Pietra performs the perfect sit/stay. Owners: R. Gravel and G. Schaffer.

THE SIT COMMAND

As with most basic commands, your puppy will learn this one in just a few lessons. You can give the puppy two lessons a day on the sit command but he will make just as much progress with one 15-minute lesson each day. Some trainers will advise you that you should not proceed to other commands until the previous one has been learned really well. However, a bright young pup is quite capable of handling more than one command per lesson, and certainly per day. Indeed, as time progresses, you will be going through each command as a matter of routine before a new one is attempted. This is so the puppy always starts, as well as ends, a lesson on a high note, having successfully completed something.

Call the puppy to you and fuss over him. Place one hand on his hindquarters and the other under his upper chest. Say "Sit" in a pleasant (never

TRAINING

harsh) voice. At the same time, push down his rear end and push up under his chest. Now lavish praise on the puppy. Repeat this a few times and your pet will get the idea. Once the puppy is in the sit position you will release your hands. At first he will tend to get up, so immediately repeat the exercise. The lesson will end when the pup is in the sit position. When the puppy understands the command, and does it right away, you can slowly move backward so that you are a few feet away from him. If he attempts to come to you, simply place him back in the original position and start again. Do not attempt to keep the pup in the sit position for too long. At this age, even a few seconds is a long while and you do not want him to get bored with lessons before he has even begun them.

THE HEEL COMMAND

All dogs should be able to walk nicely on a leash without their owners being involved in a tug-of-war. The heel command will follow leash training. Heel training is best done where you have a wall to one side of you. This will restrict the puppy's lateral movements, so you only have to contend with forward and backward situations. A fence is an

The heel exercise can teach your dog to walk beside you without pulling, which will make your daily outings together more enjoyable.

TRAINING

alternative, or you can do the lesson in the garage. Again, it is better to do the lesson in private, not on a public sidewalk where there will be many distractions.

With a puppy, there will be no need to use a choke collar as you can be just as effective with a regular one. The leash should be of good length, certainly not too short. You can adjust the space between you, the puppy, and the wall so your pet has only a small amount of room to move sideways. This being so, he will either hang back or pull ahead—the latter is the more desirable state as it indicates a bold pup who is not frightened of you.

Hold the leash in your right hand and pass it through your left. As the puppy moves ahead and strains on the leash, give the leash a quick jerk backwards with your left hand, at the same time saying "Heel." The position you want the pup to be in is such that his chest is level with, or just behind, an imaginary line from your knee. When the puppy is in this position, praise him and begin walking again, and the whole exercise will be repeated. Once the puppy begins to get the message, you can use your left hand to pat the side of your knee so the pup is encouraged to keep close to your side.

It is useful to suddenly do an about-turn when the pup understands the basics. The puppy will now be behind you, so you can pat your knee and say "Heel." As soon as the pup is in the correct position, give him lots of praise. The puppy will now be beginning to associate certain words with certain actions. Whenever he is not in the heel position he will experience displeasure as you jerk the leash, but when he comes alongside you he will receive praise. Given these two options, he will always prefer the latter—assuming he has no other reason to fear you, which would then create a dilemma in his mind.

Once the lesson has been well learned, then you can adjust your pace from a slow walk to a quick one and the puppy will come to adjust. The slow walk is always the more difficult for most puppies, as they are usually anxious to be on the move.

If you have no wall to walk against then things will be a little more difficult because the pup will tend to wander to his left. This means you need to give lateral jerks as well as bring the pup to your side. End the lesson when the pup is walking nicely

TRAINING

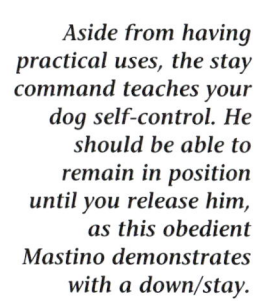

Aside from having practical uses, the stay command teaches your dog self-control. He should be able to remain in position until you release him, as this obedient Mastino demonstrates with a down/stay.

beside you. Begin the lesson with a few sit commands (which he understands by now), so you're starting with success and praise. If your puppy is nervous on the leash, you should never drag him to your side as you may see so many other people do (who obviously didn't invest in a good book like you did!). If the pup sits down, call him to your side and give lots of praise. The pup must always come to you because he wants to. If he is dragged to your side he will see you doing the dragging—a big negative. When he races ahead he does not see you jerk the leash, so all he knows is that something restricted his movement and, once he was in a given position, you gave him lots of praise. This is using canine psychology to your advantage.

Always try to remember that if a dog must be disciplined, then try not to let him associate the discipline with you. This is not possible in all matters but, where it is, this is definitely to be preferred.

THE STAY COMMAND

This command follows from the sit. Face the puppy and say "Sit." Now step backwards, and as you do, say "Stay." Let the pup remain in the position for only a few seconds before calling him to you and giving lots of praise. Repeat this, but step further back. You do not need to shout at the puppy. Your pet is not deaf; in fact, his hearing is far better than yours. Speak just loudly enough for the pup to

TRAINING

hear, yet use a firm voice. You can stretch the word to form a "sta-a-a-y." If the pup gets up and comes to you simply lift him up, place him back in the original position, and start again. As the pup comes to understand the command, you can move further and further back.

The next test is to walk away after placing the pup. This will mean your back is to him, which will tempt him to follow you. Keep an eye over your shoulder, and the minute the pup starts to move, spin around and, using a sterner voice, say either "Sit" or "Stay." If the pup has gotten quite close to you, then, again, return him to the original position.

As the weeks go by you can increase the length of time the pup is left in the stay position—but two to three minutes is quite long enough for a puppy. If your puppy drops into a lying position and is clearly more comfortable, there is nothing wrong with this. Likewise, your pup will want to face the direction in which you walked off. Some trainers will insist that the dog faces the direction he was placed in, regardless of whether you move off on his blind side. I have never believed in this sort of obedience because it has no practical benefit.

THE DOWN COMMAND

From the puppy's viewpoint, the down command can be one of the more difficult ones to accept. This is because the position is one taken up by a submissive dog in a wild pack situation. A timid dog will roll over—a natural gesture of submission. A bolder pup will want to get up, and might back off, not feeling he should have to submit to this command. He will feel that he is under attack from you and about to be punished—which is what would be the position in his natural environment. Once he comes to understand this is not the case, he will accept this unnatural position without any problem.

You may notice that some dogs will sit very quickly, but will respond to the down command more slowly—it is their way of saying that they will obey the command, but under protest!

There two ways to teach this command. One is, in my mind, more intimidating than the other, but it is up to you to decide which one works best for you. The first method is to stand in front of your puppy and bring him to the sit position, with his collar and leash on. Pass the leash under your left foot so that

TRAINING

when you pull on it, the result is that the pup's neck is forced downwards. With your free left hand, push the pup's shoulders down while at the same time saying "Down." This is when a bold pup will instantly try to back off and wriggle in full protest. Hold the pup firmly by the shoulders so he stays in the position for a second or two, then tell him what a good dog he is and give him lots of praise. Repeat this only a few times in a lesson because otherwise the puppy will get bored and upset over this command. End with an easy command that brings back the pup's confidence.

The second method, and the one I prefer, is done as follows: Stand in front of the pup and then tell him to sit. Now kneel down, which is immediately far less intimidating to the puppy than to have you towering above him. Take each of his front legs and pull them forward, at the same time saying "Down." Release the legs and quickly apply light pressure on the shoulders with your left hand. Then, as quickly, say "Good boy" and give lots of fuss. Repeat two or three times only. The pup will learn over a few lessons. Remember, this is a very

Learning good manners and obedience skills can help ensure that your Mastino will become a treasured member of the family for years to come. Owner: S. Pleplowski.

TRAINING

submissive act on the pup's behalf, so there is no need to rush matters.

RECALL TO HEEL COMMAND

When your puppy is coming to the heel position from an off-leash situation—such as if he has been running free—he should do this in the correct manner. He should pass behind you and take up his position and then sit. To teach this command, have the pup in front of you in the sit position with his collar and leash on. Hold the leash in your right hand. Give him the command to heel, and pat your left knee. As the pup starts to move forward, use your right hand to guide him behind you. If need be you can hold his collar and walk the dog around the back of you to the desired position. You will need to repeat this a few times until the dog understands what is wanted.

When he has done this a number of times, you can try it without the collar and leash. If the pup comes up toward your left side, then bring him to the sit position in front of you, hold his collar and walk him around the back of you. He will eventually understand and automatically pass around your back each time. If the dog is already behind you when you recall him, then he should automatically come to your left side, which you will be patting with your hand.

Opposite: Training your Mastino is a learning process that requires time, patience, and dedication.

THE NO COMMAND

This is a command that must be obeyed every time without fail. There are no halfway stages, he must be 100-percent reliable. Most delinquent dogs have never been taught this command; included in these are the jumpers, the barkers, and the biters. Were your puppy to approach a poisonous snake or any other potential danger, the no command, coupled with the recall, could save his life. You do not need to give a specific lesson for this command because it will crop up time and again in day-to-day life.

If the puppy is chewing a slipper, you should approach the pup, take hold of the slipper, and say "No" in a stern voice. If he jumps onto the furniture, lift him off and say "No" and place him gently on the floor. You must be consistent in the use of the command and apply it every time he is doing something you do not want him to do.

TRAINING

SHOWING YOUR NEAPOLITAN MASTIFF

You have bought a show-potential puppy, feel that he is of correct breed type, and want to put him in a dog show. First, you must gain some specialized training for you and your dog. Most dog training centers offer handling classes. The instructor will teach you the proper gaiting patterns that are used at dog shows. He will also show you how to stack your dog correctly, along with other handling tips and techniques.

Here in the United States, it is common for owners to hire a professional handler to take their dog in the ring. Some people feel that it is unfair to use a professional handler, because they always beat an owner-handler and his dog. You may find this to be true only if both dogs are of equal quality. There are some specific reasons why this can happen. The professional handler has more experience and rarely makes a mistake. He is able to choose from many good-quality dogs and he knows how to show off their good qualities. As an owner-handler, you must practice daily so that you, too, rarely make mistakes. Go to a dog show without your dog so you can watch these professionals and learn. Contrary to the belief of some people who are generally poor sportsmen, a judge will rarely put up a dog of lesser quality just because he is shown by a professional handler. If you choose to use a professional handler, you can usually meet the handler at the show site or you may board your dog with the handler. Be prepared to pay a reasonable boarding charge, handling fees, entry fees, and sometimes travel expenses.

SHOWING

When competing in conformation events, your Neapolitan Mastiff will be judged on how closely he resembles the standard of the breed. Ch. Vanguard's Adriana, owned by Gonnie Schaffer.

Your dog must have full registration and not be spayed or neutered in order to compete. A male must also have both testicles fully descended, and he must also be well socialized. The judge will probably excuse you from the ring if your dog shows aggression.

When it comes to judging, the Neapolitan Mastiff is one of the easiest dogs in which to judge breed type. Because of his distinctive characteristics, even a novice to the breed can pick between a dog that possesses good breed type and one that does not. That is not to say that it is easy to judge two or more dogs that are of good breed type. This task takes a great deal of expertise and breed knowledge. A judge must take the whole dog into consideration when awarding ribbons—movement, breed type, and soundness. A dog of excellent soundness and poor breed type should not be chosen over a dog with good breed

SHOWING

type that lacks a little soundness or proper movement. Neither should a dog be chosen because he has one or two overdone qualities when all else is lacking. The Neapolitan Mastiff is not a spectacle, and we should not select for one exaggerated body feature while losing all else. There are too many people that believe soundness is more important than breed type. Please do not interpret that this gives you permission to breed an unsound dog. Any dog that is truly unsound should be disqualified from the show ring. Just remember that without breed type, you no longer have a Neapolitan Mastiff.

Before going to a dog show there are a few items you may need to bring: paper towels and plastic bags for waste cleanup, a dog crate, a tarp used as a sun screen, bowls, food, and plenty of water. Extra caution must be taken during summer outdoor shows. You must be constantly on guard for heat exhaustion in your dog. While waiting for your dog to enter the show, keep him under the shaded tent at all times. If you see any signs of heat exhaustion, you must wet him down with a towel soaked in water. Don't hesitate; leave the show at once and get your dog to the veterinarian immediately.

Remember to dress and act professionally. When you are at a dog show, you and your dog are representatives of your breed. They say that a dog looks like his owner and if you come to a dog show dressed in shabby attire, people will think that your dog is shabby and unkempt.

In order to compete, your Mastino must have full registration documents and not be spayed or neutered.

BREEDING AND HEALTH CONCERNS

Before deciding to breed Neapolitan Mastiffs, you should study the up-to-date standard of the breed and spend up to two years researching and gathering information on the different bloodlines. Milo and his father, Ulisse, owned by G. Schaffer.

We could dedicate an entire book to dog breeding and health concerns. Breeding is an art that combines genetic principles with years of sometimes painfully acquired knowledge. Because there are numerous well-written books on this subject, we will give you a brief overview and limit our content to the ways that breeding the Neapolitan Mastiff may differ from other breeds of dog. A long-time dog breeder friend once said, "A lot of knowledge and a little luck is the secret to breeding a top-quality show dog."

BREEDING AND HEALTH CONCERNS

Today, we see some of the same problems occurring that trace back to the original dogs used to reconstruct the breed. We must be aware of problems such as long muzzles, narrow heads, incorrect heights, and light bones. If it is left up to natural selection, these problems will cause a great variation in breed type.

There are many questions you should consider before embarking on breeding:

1) Are you financially able to spend the money that it takes to purchase the best-quality foundation stock possible?

2) Are you ready for breeding, caring for puppies, and selling them? This includes bottle feeding orphan puppies every three hours or bottle feeding puppies that the mother rejects, or bottle feeding puppies if the mother does not have enough milk.

3) Are you prepared to stand behind what you have bred? This may include returning money, replacing a puppy with another one, or taking back any and all puppies you have produced if the owners can no longer keep them.

4) Are you set up to provide a home for those puppies that you do not sell? You may have a couple of puppies that you cannot sell and may have to keep them until you find them a home.

5) Do you actually have enough knowledge of the breed to be able to evaluate a litter and know which ones to keep in your breeding program?

6) Are you mentally prepared to cull those puppies that may have physical disabilities?

7) Can you afford the fee for docking and cropping ears? (Be aware that this is not permitted in some countries.)

8) Are you able to provide veterinary care for both the bitch and litter?

All of these points should be considered well in advance before the first puppy is purchased.

You must also consider what will happen to your dogs after they have passed their prime breeding age. Will you keep them or place them in a pet home? This latter possibility is the harder one, because few people seem to want to adopt older dogs.

Just a few words on mental toughness because most people find it hard to deal with the thought of their dog dying. You will have to prepare yourself for the day that one of your young show/breed prospects dies from some genetic problem that you were not aware existed. Also, the dogs that you started out with

BREEDING AND HEALTH CONCERNS

It is always important to be aware of breed-specific health and breeding concerns and the specific problems particular to large-breed dogs.

will become older and begin to pass away. This is inevitable, and the sooner you prepare yourself for these events, the better.

If breeding the Neapolitan Mastiff were as easy as placing two dogs in the same vicinity, waiting nine weeks, and presto, you'd have a perfect litter (type and soundness), then everyone would have the ultimate Mastino. Breeding is a little more involved than that.

Before breeding, you must take at least one to two years to gather as much information on the different bloodlines as possible. Acquire the up-to-date breed standard and know that standard from memory. This will help you to distinguish a good Mastino from a bad one. You should also visit numerous kennels to get to know the different lines or what several different lines look like when combined.

Also, you should gather as much medical and genetic information on the different lines as possible. Ask specific questions about the medical problems that the breeder is having with his dogs. It is up to the veracity of the breeder that you are working with to give you all of the necessary information. Make sure that your research is extensive. Find some veterinary books to read and study the following problems:

1) Canine hip dysplasia;
2) Immune system problems (Demodex);
3) Cryptorchidism or monorchidism problems;
4) Heart problems (cardiomyopathy);

BREEDING AND HEALTH CONCERNS

5) Cleft palates, harelips, or bad tail problems;
6) Ununited unconeal process problems;
7) Hypothyroidism;
8) Cherry eye.

These are some of the possible health problems that can occur with the Neapolitan Mastiff, but by no means are these problems strictly Mastino problems (most large-breed dogs have these same health problems). At the end of this section, you will find some information on a few of these health concerns.

Next, decide how many dogs you should keep in your breeding program. The number of dogs you decide to keep depends on your financial situation and whether or not you can provide adequate housing, food, veterinary care, etc. Remember that for every dog kept, you may spend up to two hours a day feeding, cleaning, and training him.

The next major concern is at what age to start breeding your stock. Males could be bred as early as one year of age, but it is advisable not to breed them until one and one-half to two years of age so that the sex organs and body are well matured. Females could be bred at one year of age, provided that they are mentally mature enough to take care of puppies, but you must wait at least until the second heat cycle before breeding her. Most breeders will not breed a dog or bitch until two years of age, at which time they are somewhat mature and all the necessary testing

Breeders may spend up to two hours a day feeding, cleaning, and training each dog in their breeding program.

BREEDING AND HEALTH CONCERNS

Most breeders will not breed a dog or bitch until two years of age, at which time the dog is somewhat mature and all of the necessary testing can be done. Ulisse Della Zacchera, a two-year-old male, shows excellent conformation.

can be done. It can be a big setback to find that your two-year-old stud dog now has a genetic problem after he has sired litters of puppies.

INBREEDING

Inbreeding consists of breedings that are very close, i.e., father to daughter, mother to son, full siblings, half brothers to half sisters. These types of breedings will result in the very best offspring or the very worst possible genetic combinations. The worst will come if you do not know all of the shortcomings of the dogs that you are dealing with. You should never inbreed when both dogs have the same serious fault. If you ascribe to these types of breedings, you must be mentally ready to cull any abnormalities. Inbreeding should only be done by the knowledgeable breeder.

LINEBREEDING

Linebreeding is the breeding of relatives, i.e., uncle to niece, aunt to nephew, first cousins, grandfather to granddaughter, and grandmother to grandson. Linebreeding is also known as breeding within a family or bloodline. In this type of breeding, you do not gather all of the negative genes immediately; you are bringing out the best without too drastically doubling up on problems. We prefer this type of breeding, and you

BREEDING AND HEALTH CONCERNS

should use linebreeding for three to four generations before using a modified outcross.

OUTCROSSING

Outcrossing consists of breeding two dogs that are totally genetically unrelated. Technically, in order to truly outcross, you need to choose a totally different breed, because all dogs in a given breed came from the same small foundation group. Looking at a pedigree, there may be no relatives in the first, second, or third generation, but looking back further in the pedigree you will find common ancestors. Most dog breeders therefore refer to an outcross as a mating with no common ancestors in the first five generations.

When linebreeding for many generations, you may have a problem or deficiency that you want to correct. An outcross breeding is then used, and a dog is selected that is dominant in that trait and produces it in his or her offspring. The resultant offspring is then bred back into your line.

Many breeders of Neapolitan Mastiffs continually outcross their dogs in order to get very big dogs (hybrid vigor). There is nothing wrong with that, but you can never fix a type that is distinctive to your dog's alone. If you continue to outcross, you end up with a hodgepodge of different looks along with different genotypes. Most of the desirable genes in the Neapolitan Mastiff are in the recessive state, and it may take several generations to lock one specific trait into your dogs. Like inbreeding, outcrossing should never be done by the novice breeder.

One reason why there are many different head styles is the failure of breeders to employ inbreeding or linebreeding consistently, thereby fixing head type. Many of the breeders here in the United States breed indiscriminately (outcrossing continually, no rhyme or reason to a breeding program), or breed to whomever is winning at the shows. Only a few breeders that employ linebreeding really know the power that this type of breeding can have for a breeding program. You must have short-term goals and long-term goals. Short-term goals focus on problems that can be corrected in a relatively short period of time. Long-term goals are ones that will take considerably more time. Also, keep in mind that if you have the same problems after five years and have not made any progress, you must reevaluate your breeding program.

BREEDING AND HEALTH CONCERNS

USNMC National Champion Justa Call Me Wally, owned by John and Rita Seibel and bred by Rene Evans.

BREEDING BASED ON PEDIGREE ALONE

As a knowledgeable breeder, you should not be breeding based on what is stated in the dog's pedigree alone. The pedigree may not always reflect the true ancestry of the dog. Some breeders have been known to substitute parents to avoid paying a stud fee. Also, since there are registries that will register a dog with little more than a handwritten pedigree, it is critical to deal with an honest breeder that uses a reputable registry. Second, just because your dog may be the grandson of a great champion, it does not ensure that he inherited his genetic makeup. You could easily select the wrong mate for this dog based on that assumption. Remember that we have only given you a tiny piece of what a breeder needs to know in order to breed the correct Neapolitan Mastiff.

BREEDING AND HEALTH CONCERNS

HYPOTHYROIDISM

The medical definition of this condition is the inability of the thyroid gland to produce adequate amounts of hormone necessary for the body to carry out normal bodily functions, and this condition could contribute to immune deficiencies.

As a breeder, you should have your dog's thyroid tested after one year of age, so that you will know how his thyroid is functioning. After the test result is returned to the veterinarian, you should keep the results in your dog's record. You should not only find out what the actual number is, but find out what is normal on the scale that is being used by the testing facility (an example of normal range is 30-50). Don't accept an answer from the veterinarian that it's low-normal, because what is okay for another breed is not okay for the Mastino. If the dog is low-normal and is one of your producing dogs, that dog should be placed on thyroid maintenance. All your dogs should be checked once a year for thyroid function. After three years of age, most Mastinos' thyroid function is not what it should be, and they may have to be placed on thyroid maintenance to maintain their breeding capabilities, even though it may be in the "normal range."

Pregnancy in females and sperm in males are luxuries of the body, and if the body lacks hormones for normal body functions, breeding capabilities will be sacrificed. That's why very typey bitches get pregnant and reabsorb their puppies or why dogs have little or no sperm at all.

CHERRY EYE

Glandular hypertrophy or "cherry eye" is a prolapse of the gland of the third eyelid. Although the cause of this condition is not yet known, it is thought to be genetic and associated with a laxity of a small ligament that holds the gland in position behind the third eyelid. Severe stress such as shipping, teething, and vaccinations may also play a role.

The gland can sometimes be manipulated back into place, but it will usually reprolapse in a few days. Some veterinary ophthalmologists may be able to successfully tack it back to the orbital rim, but there is still a fair risk of failure, even for the skilled specialist (10-50 percent). To cut out and remove the part of the gland that is sticking out is recommended and also the least expensive option. The removal of this gland can cause the eye to become dry and you may need to

BREEDING AND HEALTH CONCERNS

place drops in the eye daily. The incidence of "dry eye" is very low because this gland of the third eyelid is only responsible for approximately 30 percent of the dog's tear production. Usually, there is some portion of the gland that remains. Unless there is damage to the main orbital lacrimal gland, adequate tear production should continue.

PAW LICKING SYNDROME

Although this is not a genetic disease, many breeders and owners see this condition in their dogs and do not know what to do about it. Licking of the paws seems to happen when a dog is in a stressful situation, lacking in exercise, or not challenged mentally, which results in boredom. Licking excessively will cause the feet to get sore, infected, and swell, causing the dog to limp.

Keeping the feet from excessive moisture will help keep this condition from occurring. You should also place toys in the kennel to keep the dog active, move the dog periodically to another kennel that was occupied, and be sure to exercise him at least 10-15 minutes a day.

If your dog does get this condition, he should be taken to a veterinarian and placed on at least antibiotics in order to fight the infection internally. The feet must be kept dry and athlete's foot spray with miconazole applied twice daily. It may be necessary to place a medi-collar on the dog so it is impossible for him to lick the feet.

Reputable breeders ensure that good health and temperament are passed down to each succeeding generation.

YOUR HEALTHY NEAPOLITAN MASTIFF

Dogs, like all other animals, are capable of contracting problems and diseases that, in most cases, are easily avoided by sound husbandry—meaning well-bred and well-cared-for animals are less prone to developing diseases and problems than are carelessly bred and neglected animals. Your knowledge of how to avoid problems is far more valuable than all of the books and advice on how to cure them. Respectively, the only person you should listen to about treatment is your vet. Veterinarians don't have all the answers, but at least they are trained to analyze and treat illnesses, and are aware of the full implications of treatments. This does not mean a few old remedies aren't good standbys when all else fails, but in most cases modern science provides the best treatments for disease.

Opposite: As a responsible Neapolitan Mastiff owner, you should have a basic understanding of the medical problems that affect the breed.

PHYSICAL EXAMS

Your puppy should receive regular physical examinations or checkups. These come in two forms. One is obviously performed by your vet, and the other is a day-to-day procedure that should be done by you. Apart from the fact the exam will highlight any problem at an early stage, it is an excellent way of socializing the pup to being handled.

To do the physical exam yourself, start at the head and work your way around the body. You are looking for any sign of lesions, or any indication of parasites on the pup. The most common parasites are fleas and ticks.

HEALTH

HEALTH

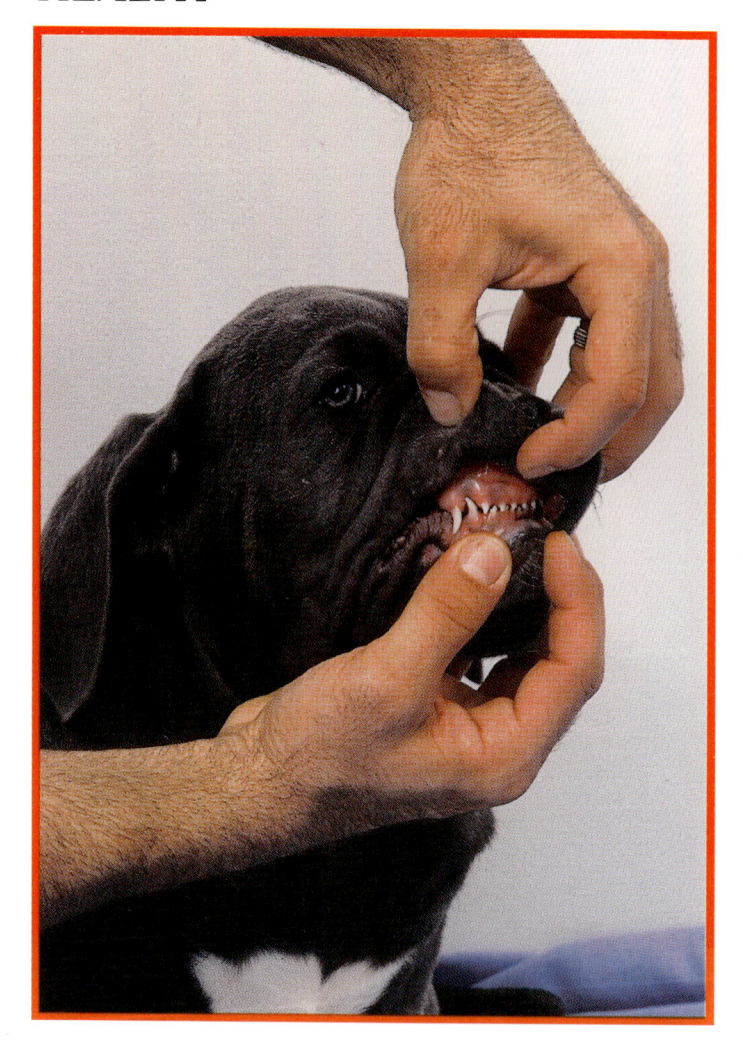

Healthy teeth and gums are important to the well-being of your Neapolitan Mastiff. Check and brush his teeth regularly.

HEALTHY TEETH AND GUMS

Chewing is instinctual. Puppies chew so that their teeth and jaws grow strong and healthy as they develop. As the permanent teeth begin to emerge, it is painful and annoying to the puppy, and puppy owners must recognize that their new charges need something safe upon which to chew. Unfortunately, once the puppy's permanent teeth have emerged and settled solidly into the jaw, the chewing instinct does not fade. Adult dogs instinctively need to clean their teeth, massage their gums, and exercise their jaws through chewing.

It is necessary for your dog to have clean teeth. You should take your dog to the veterinarian at least once a year to have his teeth cleaned and to have his mouth examined for any sign of oral disease. Although dogs do not get cavities in the same way humans do, dogs'

HEALTH

The Hercules™ by Nylabone® has raised dental tips that help fight plaque on your Mastino's teeth.

Raised dental tips on the surface of every Plaque Attacker™ help to combat plaque and tartar.

teeth accumulate tartar, and more quickly than humans do! Veterinarians recommend brushing your dog's teeth daily. But who can find time to brush their dog's teeth daily? The accumulation of tartar and plaque on our dog's teeth when not removed can cause irritation and eventually erode the enamel and finally destroy the teeth. Advanced cases, while destroying the teeth, bring on gingivitis and periodontitis, two very serious conditions that can affect the dog's internal organs as well...to say nothing about bad breath!

Since everyone can't brush their dog's teeth daily or get to the veterinarian often enough for him to scale

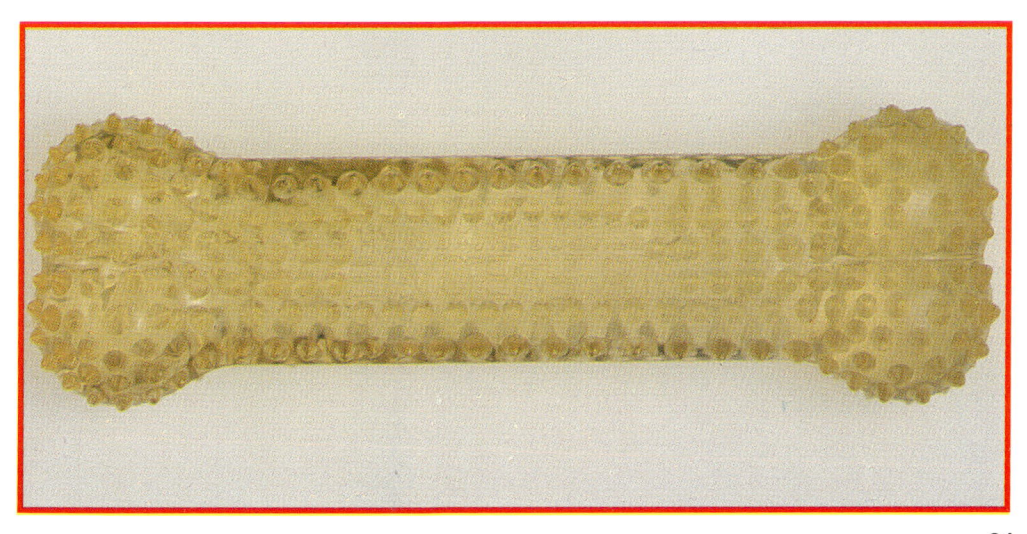

HEALTH

the dog's teeth, providing the dog with something safe to chew on will help maintain oral hygeine. Chew devices from Nylabone® keep dogs' teeth clean, but they also provide an excellent resource for entertainment and relief of doggie tensions. Nylabone® products give your dog something to do for an hour or two every day and during that hour or two, your dog will be taking an active part in keeping his teeth and gums healthy…without even realizing it! That's invaluable to your dog, and valuable to you!

Nylabone® provides fun bones, challenging bones, and *safe* bones. It is an owner's responsibility to recognize safe chew toys from dangerous ones. Your dog will chew and devour anything you give him. Dogs must not be permitted to chew on items that they can break. Pieces of broken objects can do internal damage to a dog, besides ripping the dog's mouth. Cheap plastic or rubber toys can cause stoppage in the intestines; such stoppages are operable only if caught immediately.

The most obvious choices, in this case, may be the worst choice. Natural beef bones were not designed for chewing and cannot take too much pressure from the sides. Due to the abrasive nature of these bones, they should be offered most sparingly. Knuckle bones, though once very popular for dogs, can be easily

Nylabone® is the only plastic dog bone made of 100 percent virgin nylon, specially processed to create a tough, durable, completely safe bone.

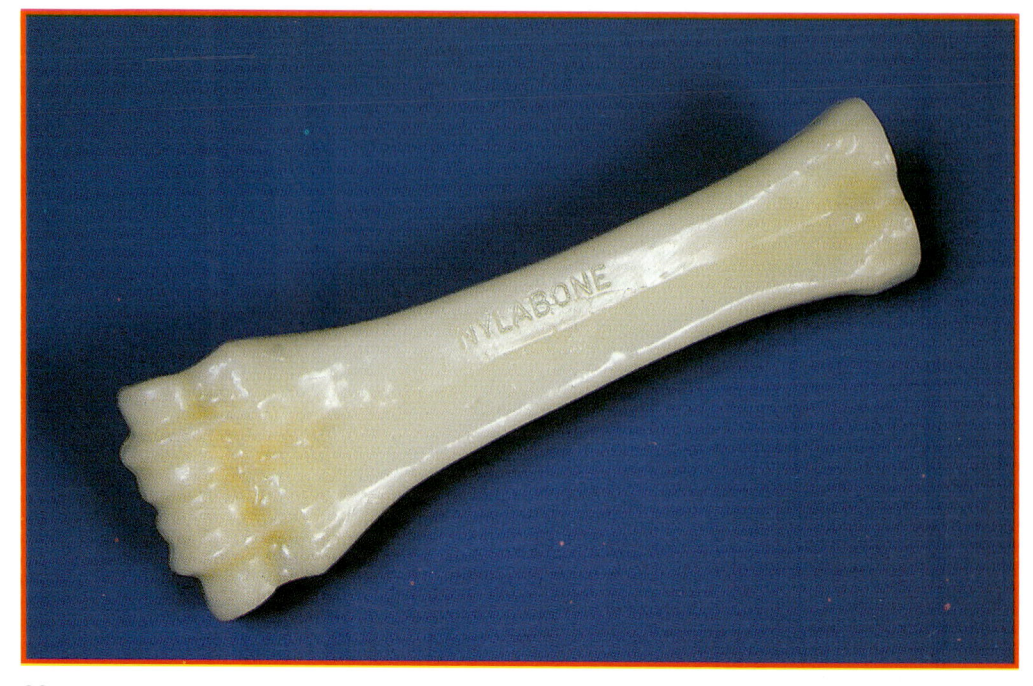

HEALTH

There are many dangers that your dog may encounter in the great outdoors, so closely supervise him when he is outside.

chewed up and eaten by dogs. At the very least, digestion is interrupted; at worst, the dog can choke or suffer from intestinal blockage.

When a dog chews hard on a Nylabone®, little bristle-like projections appear on the surface of the bone. These help to clean the dog's teeth and add to the gum-massaging. Given the chemistry of the nylon, the bristle can pass through the dog's intestinal tract without effect. Since nylon is inert, no microorganism can grow on it, and it can be washed in soap and water or sterilized in boiling water or in an autoclave.

For the sake of your dog, his teeth and your own peace of mind, provide your dog with Nylabones®. They have 100 variations from which to choose.

FIGHTING FLEAS

Fleas are very mobile and may be red, black, or brown in color. The adults suck the blood of the host, while the larvae feed on the feces of the adults, which is rich in blood. Flea "dirt" may be seen on the pup as very tiny clusters of blackish specks that look like freshly ground pepper. The eggs of fleas may be laid

HEALTH

on the puppy, though they are more commonly laid off the host in a favorable place, such as the bedding. They normally hatch in 4 to 21 days, depending on the temperature, but they can survive for up to 18 months if temperature conditions are not favorable. The larvae are maggot-like and molt a couple of times before forming pupae, which can survive long periods until the temperature, or the vibration of a nearby host, causes them to emerge and jump on a host.

There are a number of effective treatments available, and you should discuss them with your veterinarian, then follow all instructions for the one you choose. Any treatment will involve a product for your puppy or dog and one for the environment, and will require diligence on your part to treat all areas and thoroughly clean your home and yard until the infestation is eradicated.

THE TROUBLE WITH TICKS

Ticks are arthropods of the spider family, which means they have eight legs (though the larvae have six). They bury their headparts into the host and gorge on its blood. They are easily seen as small grain-like creatures sticking out from the skin. They are often picked up when dogs play in fields, but may also arrive in your yard via wild animals—even birds—or stray cats and dogs. Some ticks are species-specific, others are more adaptable and will host on many species.

The cat flea is the most common flea of dogs. It starts feeding soon after it makes contact with the dog.

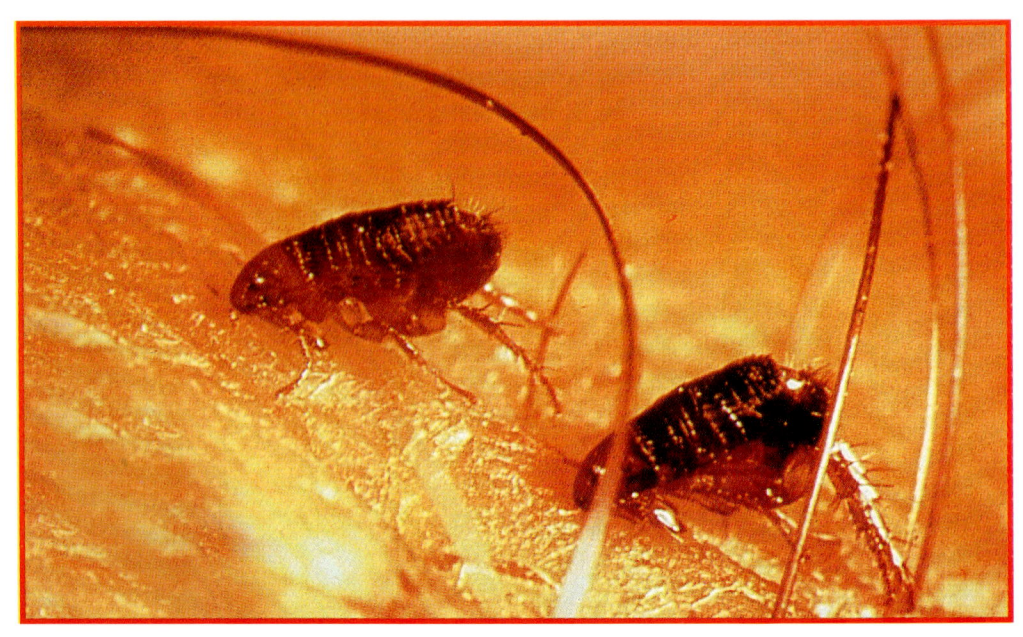

HEALTH

The deer tick is the most common carrier of Lyme disease. Photo courtesy of Virbac Laboratories, Inc., Fort Worth, Texas.

The most troublesome type of tick is the deer tick, which spreads the deadly Lyme disease that can cripple a dog (or a person). Deer ticks are tiny and very hard to detect. Often, by the time they're big enough to notice, they've been feeding on the dog for a few days—long enough to do their damage. Lyme disease was named for the area of the United States in which it was first detected—Lyme, Connecticut—but has now been diagnosed in almost all parts of the US. Your veterinarian can advise you of the danger to your dog(s) in your area, and may suggest your dog be vaccinated for Lyme. Always go over your dog with a fine-toothed flea comb when you come in from walking through any area that may harbor deer ticks, and if your dog is acting unusually sluggish or sore, seek veterinary advice.

Attempts to pull a tick free will invariably leave the headpart in the pup, where it will die and cause an infected wound or abscess. The best way to remove ticks is to dab a strong saline solution, iodine, or alcohol on them. This will numb them, causing them to loosen their hold, at which time they can be removed with forceps. The wound can then be cleaned and covered with an antiseptic ointment. If ticks are common in your area, consult with your vet for a suitable pesticide to be used in kennels, on bedding, and on the puppy or dog.

INSECTS AND OTHER OUTDOOR DANGERS

There are many biting insects, such as mosquitoes, that can cause discomfort to a puppy. Many

HEALTH

diseases are transmitted by the males of these species.

A pup can easily get a grass seed or thorn lodged between his pads or in the folds of his ears. These may go unnoticed until an abscess forms.

This is where your daily check of the puppy or dog will do a world of good. If your puppy has been playing in long grass or places where there may be thorns, pine needles, wild animals, or parasites, the checkup is a wise precaution.

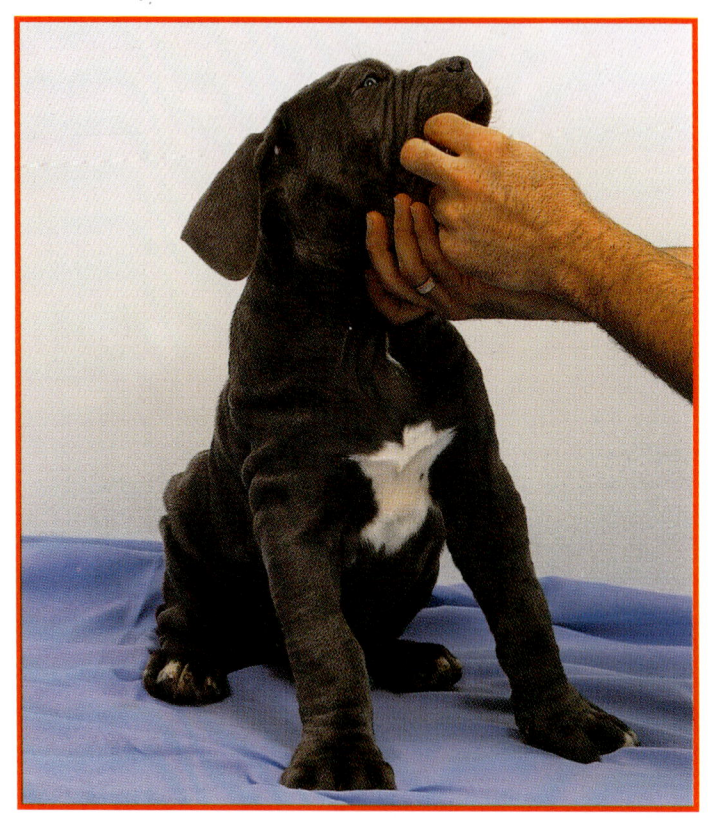

A daily checkup can help you to stay on top of your Mastino's physical condition, as well as increase the communication between you and your pet.

SKIN DISORDERS

Apart from problems associated with lesions created by biting pests, a puppy may fall foul to a number of other skin disorders. Examples are ringworm, mange, and eczema. Ringworm is not caused by a worm, but is a fungal infection. It manifests itself as a sore-looking bald circle. If your puppy should have any form of bald patches, let your veterinarian check him over; a microscopic examination can confirm the condition. Many old remedies for ringworm exist, such as iodine, carbolic acid, formalin, and other tinctures, but modern drugs are superior.

HEALTH

Fungal infections can be very difficult to treat, and even more difficult to eradicate, because of the spores. These can withstand most treatments, other than burning, which is the best thing to do with bedding once the condition has been confirmed.

Mange is a general term that can be applied to many skin conditions where the hair falls out and a flaky crust develops and falls away.

Often, dogs will scratch themselves, and this invariably is worse than the original condition, for it opens lesions that are then subject to viral, fungal, or parasitic attack. The cause of the problem can be various species of mites. These either live on skin debris and the hair follicles, which they destroy, or they bury themselves just beneath the skin and feed on the tissue. Applying general remedies from pet stores is not recommended because it is essential to identify the type of mange before a specific treatment is effective.

Eczema is another nonspecific term applied to many skin disorders. The condition can be brought about in many ways. Sunburn, chemicals, allergies to foods, drugs, pollens, and even stress can all produce a deterioration of the skin and coat. Given the range of causal factors, treatment can be difficult because the problem is one of identification. It is a case of taking each possibility at a time and trying to correctly diagnose the matter. If the cause is of a dietary nature then you must remove one item at a time in order to find out if the dog is allergic to a given food. It could, of course, be the lack of a nutrient that is the problem, so if the condition persists, you should consult your veterinarian.

INTERNAL DISORDERS

It cannot be overstressed that it is very foolish to attempt to diagnose an internal disorder without the advice of a veterinarian. Take a relatively common problem such as diarrhea. It might be caused by nothing more serious than the puppy hogging a lot of food or eating something that it has never previously eaten. Conversely, it could be the first indication of a potentially fatal disease. It's up to your veterinarian to make the correct diagnosis.

The following symptoms, especially if they accompany each other or are progressively added to earlier symptoms, mean you should visit the veterinarian right away:

HEALTH

Continual vomiting. All dogs vomit from time to time and this is not necessarily a sign of illness. They will eat grass to induce vomiting. It is a natural cleansing process common to many carnivores. However, continued vomiting is a clear sign of a problem. It may be a blockage in the pup's intestinal tract, it may be induced by worms, or it could be due to any number of diseases.

Diarrhea. This, too, may be nothing more than a temporary condition due to many factors. Even a change of home can induce diarrhea, because this often stresses the pup, and invariably there is some change in the diet. If it persists more than 48 hours then something is amiss. If blood is seen in the feces, waste no time at all in taking the dog to the vet.

Running eyes and/or nose. A pup might have a chill and this will cause the eyes and nose to weep. Again, this should quickly clear up if the puppy is placed in a warm environment and away from any drafts. If it does not, and especially if a mucous discharge is seen, then the pup has an illness that must be diagnosed.

Coughing. Prolonged coughing is a sign of a problem, usually of a respiratory nature.

Wheezing. If the pup has difficulty breathing and makes a wheezing sound when breathing, then something is wrong.

Cries when attempting to defecate or urinate. This might only be a minor problem due to the hard state of the feces, but it could be more serious, especially if the pup cries when urinating.

Cries when touched. Obviously, if you do not handle a puppy with care he might yelp. However, if he cries even when lifted gently, then he has an internal problem that becomes apparent when pressure is applied to a given area of the body. Clearly, this must be diagnosed.

Refuses food. Generally, puppies and dogs are greedy creatures when it comes to feeding time. Some might be more fussy, but none should refuse more than one meal. If they go for a number of hours without showing any interest in their food, then something is not as it should be.

General listlessness. All puppies have their off days when they do not seem their usual cheeky, mischievous selves. If this condition persists for more than two days then there is little doubt of a problem. They may not show any of the signs listed, other than

HEALTH

perhaps a reduced interest in their food. There are many diseases that can develop internally without displaying obvious clinical signs. Blood, fecal, and other tests are needed in order to identify the disorder before it reaches an advanced state that may not be treatable.

WORMS

There are many species of worms, and a number of these live in the tissues of dogs and most other animals. Many create no problem at all, so you are not even aware they exist. Others can be tolerated in small levels, but become a major problem if they number more than a few. The most common types seen in dogs are roundworms and tapeworms. While roundworms are the greater problem, tapeworms require an intermediate host so are more easily eradicated.

Roundworms are spaghetti-like worms that cause a pot-bellied appearance and dull coat, along with more severe symptoms, such as diarrhea and vomiting. Photo courtesy of Merck AgVet.

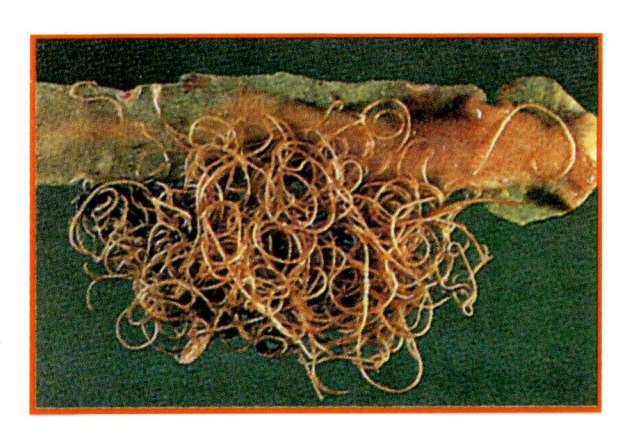

Roundworms of the species *Toxocara canis* infest the dog. They may grow to a length of 8 inches (20 cm) and look like strings of spaghetti. The worms feed on the digesting food in the pup's intestines. In chronic cases the puppy will become pot-bellied, have diarrhea, and will vomit. Eventually, he will stop eating, having passed through the stage when he always seems hungry. The worms lay eggs in the puppy and these pass out in his feces. They are then either ingested by the pup, or they are eaten by mice, rats, or beetles. These may then be eaten by the puppy and the life cycle is complete.

Larval worms can migrate to the womb of a pregnant bitch, or to her mammary glands, and this is how they pass to the puppy. The pregnant bitch can be wormed, which will help. The pups can, and should,

HEALTH

Whipworms are hard to find unless you strain your dog's feces, and this is best left to a veterinarian. Pictured here are adult whipworms.

be wormed when they are about two weeks old. Repeat worming every 10 to 14 days and the parasites should be removed. Worms can be extremely dangerous to young puppies, so you should be sure the pup is wormed as a matter of routine.

Tapeworms can be seen as tiny rice-like eggs sticking to the puppy's or dog's anus. They are less destructive, but still undesirable. The eggs are eaten by mice, fleas, rabbits, and other animals that serve as intermediate hosts. They develop into a larval stage and the host must be eaten by the dog in order to complete the chain. Your vet will supply a suitable remedy if tapeworms are seen or suspected. There are other worms, such as hookworms and whipworms, that are also blood suckers. They will make a pup anemic, and blood might be seen in the feces, which can be examined by the vet to confirm their presence. Cleanliness in all matters is the best preventative measure for all worms.

Heartworm infestation in dogs is passed by mosquitoes but can be prevented by a monthly (or daily) treatment that is given orally. Talk to your vet about the risk of heartworm in your area.

BLOAT (GASTRIC DILATATION)

This condition has proved fatal in many dogs, especially large and deep-chested breeds, such as the Weimaraner and the Great Dane. However, any dog can get bloat. It is caused by swallowing air during exercise, food/water gulping or another strenuous task. As many believe, it is not the result of flatulence. The stomach of an affected dog twists, disallowing

HEALTH

food and blood flow and resulting in harmful toxins being released into the bloodstream. Death can easily follow if the condition goes undetected.

The best preventative measure is not to feed large meals or exercise your puppy or dog immediately after he has eaten. Veterinarians recommend feeding three smaller meals per day in an elevated feeding rack, adding water to dry food to prevent gulping, and not offering water during mealtimes.

VACCINATIONS

Every puppy, purebred or mixed breed, should be vaccinated against the major canine diseases. These are distemper, leptospirosis, hepatitis, and canine parvovirus. Your puppy may have received a temporary vaccination against distemper before you purchased him, but be sure to ask the breeder to be sure.

The age at which vaccinations are given can vary, but will usually be when the pup is 8 to 12 weeks old. By this time any protection given to the pup by antibodies received from his mother via her initial milk feeds will be losing their strength.

The puppy's immune system works on the basis that the white blood cells engulf and render harmless

Rely on your veterinarian for the most effective vaccination schedule for your Neapolitan Mastiff puppy.

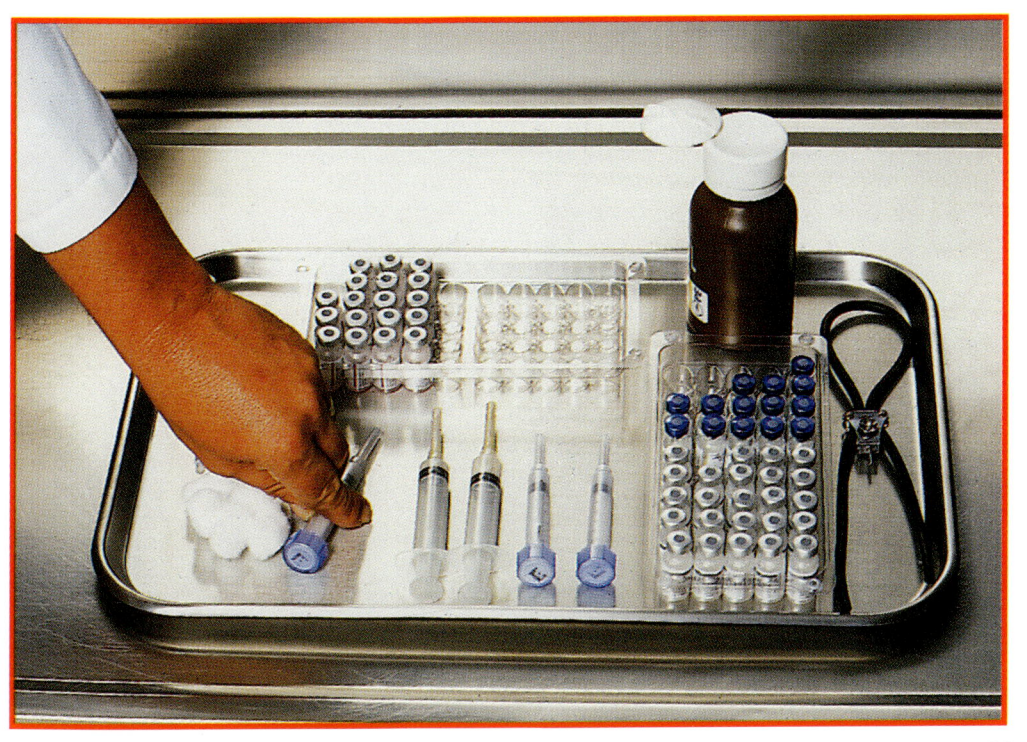

HEALTH

attacking bacteria. However, they must first recognize a potential enemy.

Vaccines are either dead bacteria or they are live, but in very small doses. Either type prompts the pup's defense system to attack them. When a large attack then comes (if it does), the immune system recognizes it and massive numbers of lymphocytes (white blood corpuscles) are mobilized to counter the attack. However, the ability of the cells to recognize these dangerous viruses can diminish over a period of time. It is therefore useful to provide annual reminders about the nature of the enemy. This is done by means of booster injections that keep the immune system on its alert. Immunization is not 100-percent guaranteed to be successful, but is very close. Certainly it is better than giving the puppy no protection.

Dogs are subject to other viral attacks, and if these are of a high-risk factor in your area, then your vet will suggest you have the puppy vaccinated against these as well.

Your puppy or dog should also be vaccinated against the deadly rabies virus. In fact, in many places it is illegal for your dog not to be vaccinated. This is to protect your dog, your family, and the rest of the animal population from this deadly virus that infects the nervous system and causes dementia and death.

ACCIDENTS

All puppies will get their share of bumps and bruises due to the rather energetic way they play. These will usually heal themselves over a few days. Small cuts should be bathed with a suitable disinfectant and then smeared with an antiseptic ointment. If a cut looks more serious, then stem the flow of blood with a towel or direct pressure and rush the pup to the veterinarian. Never apply so much pressure to the wound that it might restrict the flow of blood to the limb.

In the case of burns you should apply cold water or an ice pack to the surface. If the burn was due to a chemical, then this must be washed away with copious amounts of water. Apply petroleum jelly, or any vegetable oil, to the burn. Trim away the hair if need be. Wrap the dog in a blanket and rush him to the vet. The pup may go into shock, depending on the severity of the burn, and this will result in a lowered blood pressure, which is dangerous and the reason the pup must receive immediate veterinary attention.

HEALTH

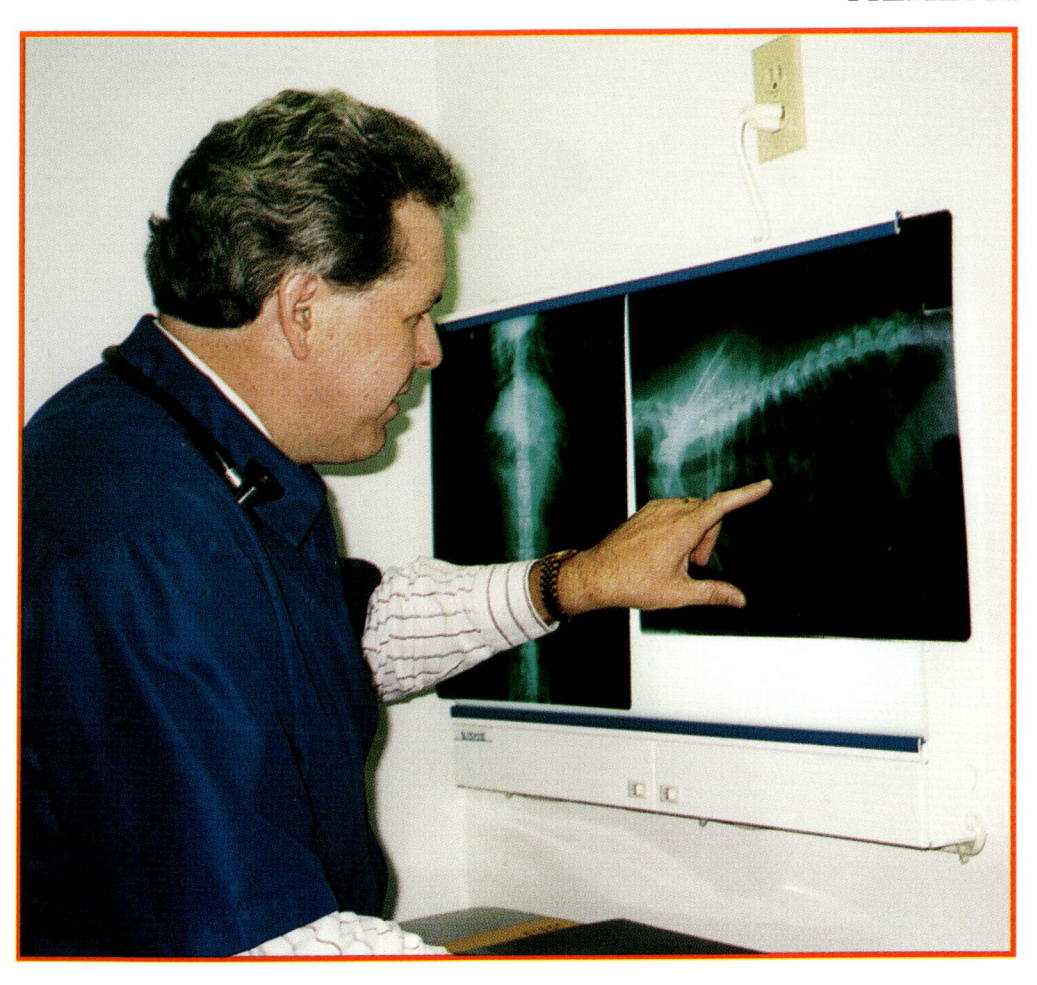

If your Neapolitan Mastiff sustains an injury from an accident or fall, acting quickly and appropriately can save his life. For example, it's a good idea to x-ray any dog hit by a car.

If a broken limb is suspected then try to keep the animal as still as possible. Wrap your pup or dog in a blanket to restrict movement and get him to the veterinarian as soon as possible. Do not move the dog's head so it is tilting backward, as this might result in blood entering the lungs.

Do not let your pup jump up and down from heights, as this can cause considerable shock to the joints. Like all youngsters, puppies do not know when enough is enough, so you must do all their thinking for them.

Provided you apply strict hygiene to all aspects of raising your puppy, and you make daily checks on his physical state, you have done as much as you can to safeguard him during his most vulnerable period. Routine visits to your veterinarian are also recommended, especially while the puppy is under one year of age. The vet may notice something that did not seem important to you.

HEAD
Large in comparison to body

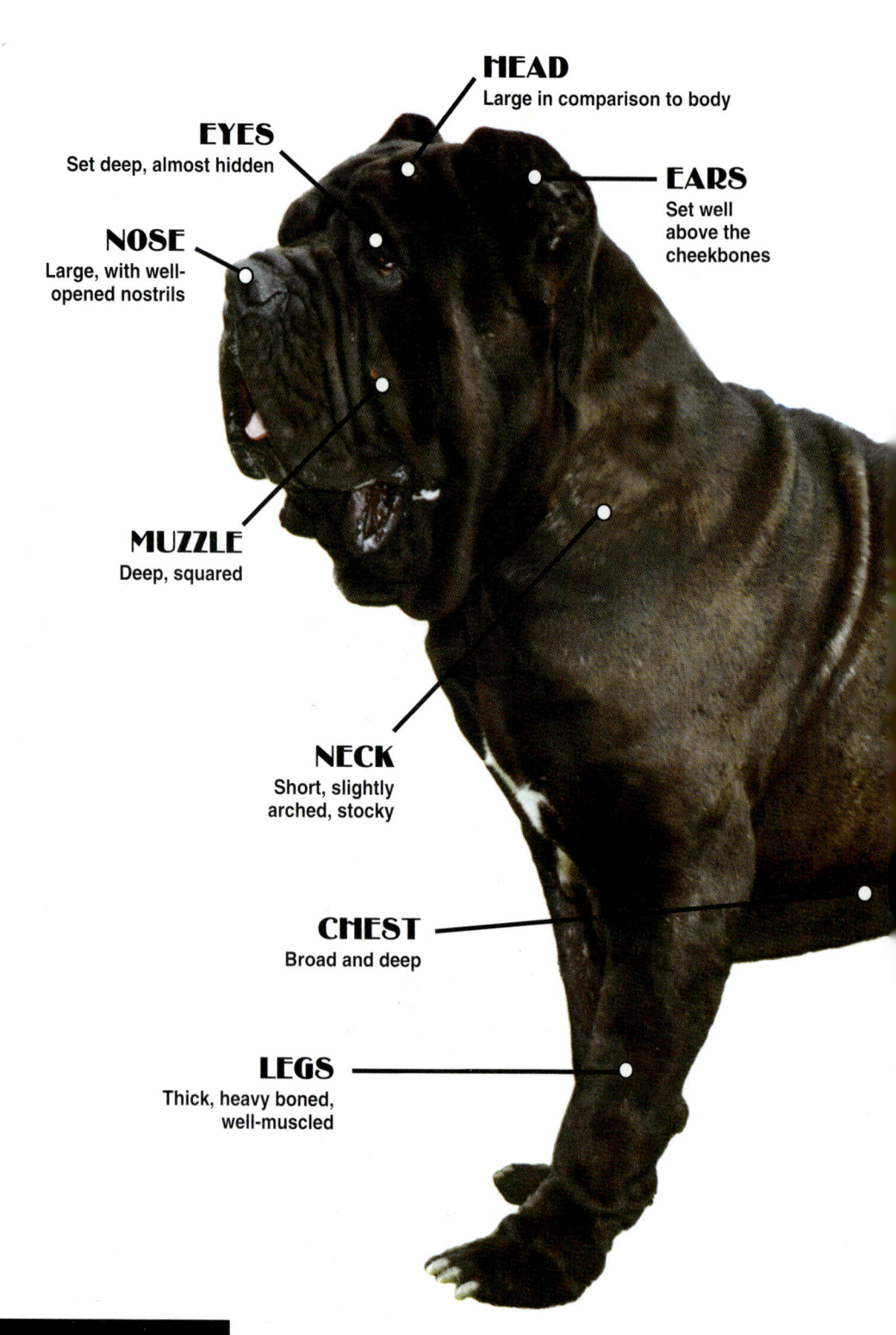

EYES
Set deep, almost hidden

EARS
Set well above the cheekbones

NOSE
Large, with well-opened nostrils

MUZZLE
Deep, squared

NECK
Short, slightly arched, stocky

CHEST
Broad and deep

LEGS
Thick, heavy boned, well-muscled

Ulisse Della Zacchera, owned by Gonnie Schaffer.